THE JUDICIAL MURDER OF MARY E. SURRATT

by
David Miller DeWitt

THE CONFEDERATE
REPRINT COMPANY
☆   ☆   ☆   ☆
WWW.CONFEDERATEREPRINT.COM

The Judicial Murder of Mary E. Surratt
by David Miller DeWitt

Originally Published in 1895
by John Murphy and Company
Baltimore, Maryland

Reprint Edition © 2014
The Confederate Reprint Company
Post Office Box 2027
Toccoa, Georgia 30577
www.confederatereprint.com

Cover and Interior Design by
Magnolia Graphic Design
www.magnoliagraphicdesign.com

ISBN-13: 978-0692293737
ISBN-10: 0692293736

Oceans of horse-hair, continents of parchment, and learned-sergeant eloquence, were it continued till the learned tongue wore itself small in the indefatigable learned mouth, cannot make the unjust just. The grand question still remains, Was the judgment just? If unjust, it will not and cannot get harbour for itself, or continue to have footing in this Universe, which was made by other than One Unjust. Enforce it by never such statuting, three readings, royal assents; blow it to the four winds with all manner of quilted trumpeters and pursuivants, in the rear of them never so many gibbets and hangmen, it will not stand, it cannot stand. From all souls of men, from all ends of Nature, from the Throne of God above, there are voices bidding it: Away! Away!

Past and Present

CONTENTS

☆ ☆ ☆ ☆

PRELIMINARY

CHAPTER ONE
    The Reign of Terror 9

CHAPTER TWO
    The Bureau of Military (In)Justice 19

PART I: THE MURDER

CHAPTER THREE
    The Opening of the Court. Was She Ironed? 27

CHAPTER FOUR
    Animus of the Judges 39

CHAPTER FIVE
    Conduct of the Trial 51

CHAPTER SIX
    Arguments of the Defense 61

CHAPTER SEVEN
    Charge of Judge Bingham 71

CHAPTER EIGHT
The Verdict, Sentence and Petition 79

CHAPTER NINE
The Death Warrant and Execution 93

CHAPTER TEN
Was It Not Murder? The Milligan Case 103

PART II: THE VINDICATION

CHAPTER ELEVEN
Setting Aside the Verdict. Discharge of Jefferson Davis . . . 119

CHAPTER TWELVE
Reversal on the Merits. Trial of John H. Surratt 133

CHAPTER THIRTEEN
The Recommendation to Mercy 145

CHAPTER FOURTEEN
The Trial of Joseph Holt 163

CHAPTER FIFTEEN
Andrew Johnson Signs Another Death Warrant 183

CHAPTER SIXTEEN
Conclusion 193

PRELIMINARY

CHAPTER ONE
The Reign of Terror

  The assassination of Abraham Lincoln burst upon the City of Washington like a black thunder-bolt out of a cloudless sky. On Monday, the 3d of April, 1865, Richmond was taken. On the succeeding Sunday (the ninth), General Lee with the main Army of the South surrendered. The Rebellion of nearly one-half the nation lay in its death-throes. The desperate struggle for the unity of the Republic was ending in a perfect triumph; and the loyal people gave full rein to their joy. Every night the streets of the city were illuminated. The chief officers of the government, one after another, were serenaded. On the evening of Tuesday, the eleventh, the President addressed his congratulations to an enthusiastic multitude from a window of the White House. On the night of Thursday (the thirteenth), Edwin M. Stanton, the Secretary of War, and Ulysses S. Grant, the victorious General of the Army of the North, were tumultuously greeted with banners and music and cannon at the residence of the Secretary. The next day, Friday the 14th, was the fourth anniversary of the surrender of Fort Sumter to the South, and that national humiliation was to be avenged by the restoration of the flag of the United States to its proper place above the fort by the hand of the same gallant officer who had been compelled to pull it down. In the evening, a torch-light procession perambulated the streets of the Federal Capital. Enthusiastic throngs filled the theatres, where the presence of great officials had been advertised by huge placards, and whose walls were everywhere festooned with the American flag. After four years of agonizing but unabating strain, all patriots felt justified in yielding to the full enjoyment of the glorious relaxation.

Suddenly, at its very zenith, the snap of a pistol dislimns and scatters this great jubilee, as though it were, indeed, the insubstantial fabric of a vision. At half past ten that night, from the box of the theatre where the President is seated, a shot is heard; a wild figure, hatless and clutching a gleaming knife, emerges through the smoke; it leaps from the box to the stage, falls upon one knee, recovers itself, utters one shout and waves aloft its bloody weapon; then turns, limps across in front of the audience and disappears like a phantom behind the scenes. Simultaneously, there breaks upon the startled air the shriek of a woman, followed close by confused cries of "Water! Water!" and "The President is shot!"

For the first few moments both audience and actors are paralyzed. One man alone jumps from the auditorium to the stage and pursues the flying apparition. But, as soon as the hopeless condition of the President and the escape of the assassin begin to transpire, angry murmurs of "Burn the Theatre!" are heard in the house, and soon swell into a roar in the street where a huge crowd has already assembled.

The intermingling throng surges into the building from every quarter, and mounts guard at every exit. Not one of the company of actors is allowed to go out. The people seem to pause for a moment, as if awaiting from Heaven a retribution as sudden and awful as the crime.

All their joy is turned to grief in the twinkling of an eye. The Rebellion they had too easily believed to be dead could still strike, it seemed, a fatal blow against the very life of the Republic. A panic seizes the multitude in and around the theatre, and from the theatre spreads, "like the Night," over the whole city. And when the frightened citizens hear, as they immediately do, the story of the bloody massacre in the house of the Secretary of State, occurring at the same hour with the murder of the President, the panic swells into a reign of terror. The wildest stories find the quickest and most eager credence. Every member of the Cabinet and the General of the Army have been, or are about to be, killed; the government itself is at a standstill; and the lately discomfited rebels are soon to be in possession of the Capital. Patriotic people, delivering themselves over to a fear of they know not what, cry hoarsely for vengeance on they know not whom. The citizen upon whose past loyalty the slightest suspicion can be cast cowers for safety close to his hearth-stone. The terror-stricken multitude want but a leader cool and unscrupulous enough, to plunge into a promiscuous slaughter, such as stained the new-born revolution in France. A leader, indeed, they soon find, but he is not a Danton. He is a leader only in the sense that he has caught the same madness of terror and suspicion which has seized the people, that he holds high place, and that he has the power and is in a fit humor to pander to the panic.

Edwin M. Stanton was forced by the tremendous crisis up to the very top of affairs. Vice-President Johnson, in the harrowing novelty of his position, was for the time being awed into passive docility. The Secretary of State was doubly disabled, if not killed. The General of the Army was absent. The Secretary of War without hesitation grasped the helm thus thrust into his hand, but, alas! he immediately lost his head. His exasperation at the irony of fate, which could so ruthlessly and in a moment wither the triumph of a great cause by so unexpected and overwhelming a calamity, was so profound and intense, his desire for immediate and commensurate vengeance was so uncontrollable and unreasoning, as to distort his perception, unsettle his judgment, and thus cause him to form an estimate of the nature and extent of the impending danger as false and exaggerated as that of the most panic-stricken wretch in the streets. Personally, besides, he was unfitted in many respects for such an emergency. Though an able and, it may be, a great War-Minister, he exerted no control over his temper; he habitually identified a conciliatory and charitable disposition with active disloyalty; and, being unpopular with the people of Washington by reason of the gruffness of his ways and the inconsistencies of his past political career, he had reached the unalterable conviction that the Capital was a nest of sympathizers with the South, and that he was surrounded by enemies of himself and his country.

When, therefore, upon the crushing news that the President was slain, followed hard the announcement that another assassin had made a slaughter-house of the residence of the Minister's own colleague, self-possession – the one supreme quality which was indispensable to a leader at such an awful juncture – forsook him and fled.

Before the breath was out of the body of the President, the Secretary had rushed to the conclusion, unsupported as yet by a shadow of testimony, that the acts of Booth and of the assailant of Seward (at the moment supposed to be John H. Surratt) were the outcome of a widespread, numerous and powerful conspiracy to kill, not only the President and the Secretary of State, but all the other heads of the Departments, the Vice-President and the General of the Army as well, and thus bring the government to an end; and that the primary moving power of the conspiracy was the defunct Rebellion as represented by its titular President and his Cabinet, and its agents in Canada. This belief, embraced with so much precipitation, immediately became more than a belief; it became a fixed idea in his mind. He saw, heard, felt and cherished every thing that favored it. He would see nothing, would hear nothing, and hated everything, that in the slightest degree militated against it. Upon this theory he began, and upon this theory he prosecuted to the end, every effort for the discovery, arrest, trial and punishment of the murderers.

He was seconded by a lieutenant well-fitted for such a purpose – General Lafayette C. Baker, Chief of the Detective Force. In one of the two minority reports presented to the House of Representatives by the Judiciary Committee, on the Impeachment Investigation of 1867, this man and his methods are thus delineated:

The first witness examined was General Lafayette C. Baker, late chief of the detective police, and although examined on oath, time and again, and on various occasions, it is doubtful whether he has in any one thing told the truth, even by accident. In every important statement he is contradicted by witnesses of unquestioned credibility. And there can be no doubt that to his many previous outrages, entitling him to an unenviable immortality, he has added that of wilful and deliberate perjury; and we are glad to know that no one member of the committee deems any statement made by him as worthy of the slightest credit. What a blush of shame will tinge the cheek of the American student in future ages, when he reads that this miserable wretch for years held, as it were, in the hollow of his hand, the liberties of the American people. That, clothed with power by a reckless administration, and with his hordes of unprincipled tools and spies permeating the land everywhere, with uncounted thousands of the people's money placed in his hands for his vile purposes, this creature not only had power to arrest without crime or writ, and imprison without limit, any citizen of the republic, but that he actually did so arrest thousands, all over the land, and filled the prisons of the country with the victims of his malice, or that of his masters.

In this man's hands Secretary Stanton placed all the resources of the War Department, in soldiers, detectives, material and money, and commanded him to push ahead and apprehend all persons suspected of complicity in the assumed conspiracy, and to conduct an investigation as to the origin and progress of the crime, upon the theory he had adopted and which, as much as any other, Baker was perfectly willing to accept and then, by his peculiar methods, establish. Forthwith was ushered in the grand carnival of detectives. Far and wide they sped. They had orders from Baker to do two things:

I. To arrest all the "Suspect." II. By promises, rewards, threats, deceit, force, or any other effectual means, to extort confessions and procure testimony to establish the conspiracy whose existence had been postulated.

At two o'clock in the morning of Saturday, the fifteenth, they burst into the house of Mrs. Surratt and displaying the bloody collar of the coat of the dying Lincoln, demanded the whereabouts of Booth and Surratt. It being presently discovered that Booth had escaped on horseback across the Navy Yard Bridge with David Herold ten minutes in his rear, a dash was made upon the livery-stables of Washington, their proprietors taken into custody, and then the whole of lower Maryland was invaded, the soldiers declaring martial law as they progressed. Ford's theatre was taken and held by an armed force, and the proprietor and employees were all swept into prison, including Edward Spangler, a scene-shifter, who had been a menial attendant of Booth's. The superstitious notion prevailed that the inanimate edifice whose walls had suffered such a desecration was in some vague sense an accomplice; the Secretary swore that no dramatic performance should ever take place there again; and the suspicion was sedulously kept alive that the manager and the whole force of the company must have aided their favorite actor, or the crime could not have been so easily perpetrated and the assassin escaped.

On the night of the fifteenth (Saturday) a locked room in the Kirkwood House, where Vice President Johnson was stopping, which had been engaged by George A. Atzerodt on the morning of the fourteenth, was broken open, and in the bed were found a bowie-knife and a revolver, and on the wall a coat (subsequently identified as Herold's), in which was found, among other articles, a bank book of Booth's. The room had not been otherwise occupied – Atzerodt, after taking possession of it, having mysteriously disappeared.

On the morning of the seventeenth (Monday), at Baltimore, Michael O'Laughlin was arrested as a friend of Booth's, and it was soon thought that he *"resembled extremely"* a certain suspicious stranger who, it was remembered, had been seen prowling about Secretary Stanton's residence on the night of the 13th, when the serenade took place, and there doing such an unusual act as inquiring for, and looking at, General Grant.

On the same day at Fort Monroe, Samuel Arnold was arrested, whose letter signed "Sam" had been found on Saturday night among the effects of Booth.

On the night of the seventeenth, also, the house of Mrs. Surratt with all its contents was taken possession of by the soldiers, and Mrs. Surratt, her daughter, and all the other inmates were taken into custody. While the ladies were making preparations for their departure to prison, a man disguised as a laborer, with a sleeve of his knit undershirt drawn over his head, a pick-axe on his shoulder, and covered with mud, came to the door with the story that he was to dig a drain for Mrs. Surratt in the morning; and that lady asseverating that she had never seen the man before, he was swept with the rest to headquarters, and there, to the astonishment of everybody, turned out to be the desperate assailant of the Sewards.

During these few days Washington was like a city of the dead. The streets were hung with crape. The obsequies, which started on its march across the continent the colossal funeral procession in which the whole people were mourners, were being celebrated with the most solemn pomp. No business was done except at Military Headquarters. Men hardly dared talk of the calamity of the nation. Everywhere soldiers and police were on the alert to seize any supposed or denounced sympathizer with the South. Mysterious and prophetic papers turned up at the White House and the War Department. Women whispered terrible stories of what they knew about the "Great Crime." To be able to give evidence was to be envied as a hero.

And still the arch-devil of the plot could not be found!

The lower parts of Maryland seethed like a boiling pot, and the prisons of Washington were choking with the "suspect" from that quarter. Lloyd – the drunken landlord of the tavern at Surrattsville, ten miles from Washington, at which Booth and Herold had stopped at midnight of the fatal Friday for carbines and whisky – after two days of stubborn denial was at last frightened into confession; and Doctor Mudd, who had set Booth's leg Saturday morning thirty miles from Washington, was in close confinement. All the intimate friends of the actor in Washington, in Baltimore, in Philadelphia, in New York and even in Montreal were in the clutches of the government. Surratt himself – the pursuit of whom, guided by Weichman, his former college-chum, his room-mate, and the favorite guest of his mother, had been instant and thorough – it was ascertained, had left Canada on the 12th of April and was back again on the 18th.

But where was Booth? where Herold? where Atzerodt?

On the 20th, the Secretary of War applied the proper stimulus by issuing a proclamation to the following effect:

> $50,000 reward will be paid by this department for the apprehension of the murderer of our late beloved President.
>
> $25,000 reward for the apprehension of John H. Surratt, one of Booth's accomplices.
>
> $25,000 reward for the apprehension of Herold, another of Booth's accomplices.
>
> Liberal rewards will be paid for any information that shall conduce to the arrest of either of the above-named criminals or their accomplices.
>
> All persons harboring or secreting the said persons, or either of them, or aiding or assisting in their concealment or escape, will be treated as accomplices in the murder of the President and the attempted assassination of the Secretary of State, and shall be subject to trial before a military commission and the punishment of death.

What is noteworthy about this document is that Stanton had already made up his mind as to the guilt of the persons named as accomplices of Booth; that he needed only their arrest, being assured of their consequent conviction; and that he had already determined that their trial and the trial of all persons connected with the great crime, however remotely, should be had before a military tribunal, and that the punishment to follow conviction should be death.

At four o'clock in the morning of the very day this proclamation was issued, Atzerodt was apprehended at the house of his cousin in Montgomery County, Maryland, about twenty-two miles northward of Washington, by a detail of soldiers, to whom, by the way, notwithstanding the arrest preceded the proclamation, $25,000 reward was subsequently paid. With Atzerodt his cousin, Richter, was taken also. O'Laughlin, Payne, Arnold, Atzerodt and Richter, as they were severally arrested, were put into the custody of the Navy Department and confined on board the Monitor *Saugus*, which on the morning of Saturday, when the President died, had been ordered to swing out into the middle of the river opposite the Navy Yard, prepared to receive at any hour, day or night, dead or alive, the arch-assassin. Each of these prisoners was loaded with double irons and kept under a strong guard. On the 23d, Atzerodt, by order of the Secretary of War, was transferred to the Monitor *Montauk*, to separate him from his cousin, and Payne, in addition to his double irons, had a ball and chain fastened to each ankle by the direction of the same officer. On the next day Spangler, who had hitherto been confined in the Old Capitol Prison, was transferred to one of the Monitors and presumably subjected to the same treatment. On the same day the following order was issued:

> The Secretary of War requests that the prisoners on board iron-clads belonging to this department for better security against conversation shall have a canvass bag put over the head of each and tied around the neck, with a hole for proper breathing and eating, but not seeing, and that Payne be secured to prevent self-destruction.

All of which was accordingly done.

And still no Booth! It seems as though the Secretary were mad enough to imagine that he could wring from Providence the arrest of the principal assassin by heaping tortures on his supposed accomplices.

At length, in the afternoon of the 26th – Wednesday, the second week after the assassination – Col. Conger arrived with the news of the death of Booth and the capture of Herold on the early morning of that day; bringing with him the diary and other articles found on the person of Booth, which were delivered to Secretary Stanton at his private residence. In the dead of the ensuing night, the body of Booth, sewed up in an old army blanket, arrived, attended by the dog-like Herold; and the living and the dead were immediately transferred to the *Montauk*. Herold was double ironed, balled and chained and hooded. The body of Booth was identified; an autopsy held; the shattered bone of his neck taken out for preservation as a relic (it now hangs from the ceiling of the Medical Museum into which Ford's Theatre was converted, or did before the collapse); and then, with the utmost secrecy and with all the mystery which could be fabricated, under the direction of Col. Baker, the corpse was hurriedly taken from the vessel into a small boat, rowed to the Arsenal grounds, and buried in a grave dug in a large cellar-like apartment on the ground floor of the Old Penitentiary; the door was locked, the key removed and delivered into the hands of Secretary Stanton. No effort was spared to conceal the time, place and circumstances of the burial. False stories were set afloat by Baker in furtherance of such purpose. Stanton seemed to fear an escape or rescue of the dead man's body; and vowed that no rebel or no rebel sympathizer should have a chance to glory over the corpse, or a fragment of the corpse, of the murderer of Lincoln.

CHAPTER TWO
The Bureau of Military (In)Justice

  Mingling with the varied emotions evoked by the capture and death of the chief criminal was a feeling of deepest exasperation that the foul assassin should after all have eluded the ignominious penalty of his crime. Thence arose a savage disposition on the part of the governing powers to wreak this baffled vengeance first, on his inanimate body; secondly, on the lives of his associates held so securely in such close custody; and thirdly, on all those in high places who might be presumed to sympathize with his deeds. It was too horrible to imagine that the ghost of the martyred Lincoln should walk unavenged. So stupendous a calamity must of necessity be the outcome of as stupendous a conspiracy, and must in the very justice of things be followed by as stupendous a retribution. A sacrifice must be offered and the victims must be forthcoming. To employ the parallel subsequently drawn by General Ewing on the trial of the conspirators: On the funeral pyre of Patroclus must be immolated the twelve Trojan captives. They were sure of Payne and of Herold. They held Arnold and O'Laughlin and Atzerodt and Spangler and Doctor Mudd – all the supposed satellites of Booth, save one. John H. Surratt could not be found. Officers in company with Weichman and Holahan, boarders at his mother's house, who in the terror of the moment had given themselves up on the morning of the fifteenth, traced him to Canada, as has already been noticed, but had there lost track of him. They had returned disappointed; and now Weichman and Holahan were in solitary confinement. Notwithstanding the large rewards out for his capture, as to him alone the all-powerful government seemed to be baffled. One consolation there was, however – if they could not find the son, they held the mother as a hostage for him, and they clung to the cruel expectation that by putting her to the torture of a trial and a sentence, they might force the son from his hiding place.

In the meanwhile the Bureau of Military Justice, presided over by Judge-Advocate-General Holt, had been unceasingly at work. General Baker with his posse of soldiers and detectives scoured the country far and wide for suspected persons and witnesses, hauled them to Washington and shut them up in the prisons. Then the Bureau of Military Justice took them in hand, and, when necessary, by promises, hopes of reward and threats of punishment, squeezed out of them the testimony they wanted. Colonel Henry L. Burnett, who had become an expert in such proceedings from having recently conducted the trial of Milligan before a military tribunal at Indianapolis, was brought on to help Judge Holt in the great and good work. In the words of General Ewing in his plea for Dr. Mudd:

> The very frenzy of madness ruled the hour. Reason was swallowed up in patriotic passion, and a feverish and intense excitement prevailed most unfavorable to a calm, correct hearing and faithful repetition of what was said, especially by the suspected. Again, and again, and again the accused was catechised by detectives, each of whom was vieing with the other as to which should make the most important discoveries, and each making the examination with a preconceived opinion of guilt, and with an eager desire, if not determination, to find in what might be said the proofs of guilt. Again, the witnesses testified under the strong stimulus of a promised reward for information leading to arrest and followed by convictions.

The Bureau conducted the investigation on the preconceived theory, adopted, as we have seen, by the Secretary of War, that the Confederate Government was the source of the conspiracy; and, by lavishing promises and rewards, it had no difficulty in finding witnesses who professed themselves to have been spies on the rebel agents in Canada and who were ready to implicate them and through them the President of the defunct Confederacy in the assassination. Richard Montgomery and Sanford Conover, who had been in personal communication with these agents during the past year, were eagerly taken into the employ of the Bureau, and made frequent trips to Canada, to return every time laden with fresh proofs of the complicity of the rebels.

To illustrate how the Bureau of Military Justice dealt with witnesses who happened to have been connected more or less closely with Booth, and who were either reluctant or unable to make satisfactory disclosures, here are two extracts from the evidence given on the trial of John H. Surratt in 1867.

The first is from the testimony of Lloyd, the besotted keeper of the Surratt tavern:

> I was first examined at Bryantown by Colonel Wells. I was next examined by two different persons at the Carroll prison. I did not know either of their names. One was a military officer. I think some of the prisoners described him as Colonel Foster. I saw a man at the conspiracy trial as one of the Judges who looked very much like him.... I told him I had made a fuller statement to Colonel Wells than I could possibly do to him under the circumstances, while things were fresh in my memory. His reply was that it was not full enough, and then commenced questioning me whether I had ever heard any person say that something wonderful or something terrible was going to take place. I told him I had never heard anyone say so. Said he I have seen it in the newspapers.
>
> He jumps up very quick off his seat, as if very mad, and asked me if I knew what I was guilty of. I told him, under the circumstances I did not. He said you are guilty as an accessory to a crime the punishment of which is death. With that I went up-

stairs to my room.

The next is from the testimony of Lewis J. Carland, to whom Weichman confessed his remorse after the execution of Mrs. Surratt:

> He [Weichman] said it would have been very different with Mrs. Surratt if he had been let alone; that a statement had been prepared for him, that it was written out for him, and that he was threatened with prosecution as one of the conspirators if he did not swear to it. He said that a detective had been put into Carroll prison with him, and that this man had written out a statement which he said he had made in his sleep, and that he had to swear to that statement.

Let us add another; it is so short and yet so suggestive. It is from the testimony of James J. Gifford, who was a witness for the prosecution on both trials.

> Q: Do you know Mr. Weichman?
> A: I have seen him.
> Q: Were you in Carroll prison with him?
> A: Yes, sir.
> Q: Did he say in your presence that an officer of the government had told him that unless he testified to more than he had already stated they would hang him too?
> A: I heard the officer tell him so.

After a fortnight of such wholesale processes of arrest, imprisonment, inquisition, reward and intimidation, the Bureau of Military Justice announced itself ready to prove the charges it had formulated. Thereupon two proclamations were issued by President Johnson. One, dated May the first, after stating that the Attorney General had given his opinion "that all persons implicated in the murder of the late President, Abraham Lincoln, and the attempted assassination of the Hon. William H. Seward, Secretary of State, and in an alleged conspiracy to assassinate other officers of the Federal Government at Washington City, and their aiders and abettors, are subject to the jurisdiction of and legally triable before a Military Commission," ordered 1st, "that the Assistant Adjutant-General (W. A. Nichols) detail nine competent military officers to serve as a Commission for the trial of said parties, and that the Judge-Advocate-General proceed to prefer charges against said parties for their alleged offences, and bring them to trial before said Military Commission." 2d, "that Brevet Major-General Hartranft be assigned to duty as Special Provost-Marshal-General for the purpose of said trial and attendance upon said Commission, and the execution of its mandates."

The other proclamation, dated May 2nd, after reciting that "it appears from evidence in the Bureau of Military Justice, that the atrocious murder of the late President, Abraham Lincoln, and the attempted assassination of the Hon. William H. Seward, Secretary of State, were incited, concerted, and procured by and between Jefferson Davis, late of Richmond, Va., and Jacob Thompson, Clement C. Clay, Beverly Tucker, George N. Sanders, William C. Cleary, and other rebels and traitors against the Government of the United States, harbored in Canada," offered the following rewards:

$100,000 for the arrest of Jefferson Davis.
$25,000 for the arrest of Clement C. Clay.
$25,000 for the arrest of Jacob Thompson, late of Mississippi.
$25,000 for the arrest of Geo. N. Saunders.
$25,000 for the arrest of Beverly Tucker.
$10,000 for the arrest of Wm. C. Cleary, late clerk of Clement C. Clay.

The Provost-Marshal-General of the United States is directed to cause a description of said persons, with notice of the above rewards, to be published.

At this date the President of the defunct Confederacy was a fugitive, without an army; and bands of U.S. Cavalry were already on the scout to intercept his flight. Military Justice, however, was too impatient to await the arrest of the prime object of its sword; and in obedience to the first proclamation proceeded without delay to organize a court to try the prisoners selected from the multitude undergoing confinement as the fittest victims to appease the shade of the murdered President. Over some of the "suspect" the Judge-Advocates for a time vacillated, whether to include them in the indictment or to use them as witnesses; but, after a season of rigid examinations, renewed and revised, they at last concluded that such persons would be more available in the latter capacity.

On the third day of May the funeral car, which, leaving Washington on the twenty-first of April, had borne the body of the lamented Lincoln through State after State, arrived at last at Springfield; and on the following day the cherished remains were there consigned to the tomb. On the sixth, by special order of the Adjutant-General, a Military Commission was appointed to meet at Washington on Monday, the eighth day of May, or as soon thereafter as practicable, "for the trial of David E. Herold, George A. Atzerodt, Lewis Payne, Michael O'Laughlin, Edward Spangler, Samuel Arnold, Mary E. Surratt, Samuel A. Mudd and such other prisoners as may be brought before it, implicated in the murder of the late President and in the attempted assassination of the Secretary of State and in an alleged conspiracy to assassinate other officers of the Federal Government at Washington City, and their aiders and abettors. By order of the President of the United States." And so, all things being in readiness, let the curtain rise.

PART I: THE MURDER

CHAPTER THREE
The Opening of the Court

On the ninth day of May the Commission met but only to adjourn that the prisoners might employ counsel. On the same day, two of its members, General Cyrus B. Comstock and Colonel Horace Porter – names to be noted for what may have been a heroic refusal – were relieved from the duty of sitting upon the Commission, and two other officers substituted in their stead.

So that Tuesday, May 10th, 1865 – twenty-six days after the assassination, a period much too short for the intense excitement and wild desire for vengeance to subside – may properly be designated as the first session of the Court. On the early morning of that day – before daylight – Jefferson Davis had been captured, and was immediately conducted, not to Washington to stand trial for his alleged complicity in the assassination, but to Fort Monroe. On the next day Clement C. Clay, also, surrendered himself to the United States authorities, and was sent, not to Washington to meet the awful charge formulated against him, but to the same military fortress.

The room in which the Commission met was in the northeast corner of the third story of the Old Penitentiary; a building standing in the U.S. Arsenal Grounds at the junction of the Potomac with the Eastern Branch, in a room on the ground floor of which the body of Booth had been secretly buried. Its windows were guarded by iron gratings, and it communicated with that part of the prison where the accused were now confined, by a door in the western wall. The male prisoners had been removed some days before from the Monitors to the Penitentiary, where Mrs. Surratt was already incarcerated, and each of them, including the lady, was now immured in a solitary cell under the surveillance of a special guard.

Around a table near the eastern side of this room sat, resplendent in full uniform, the members of the Court. At the head as President was Major-General David Hunter – a stern, white-headed soldier, sixty-three years old; a fierce radical; the first officer to organize the slaves into battalions of war; the warm personal friend of Lincoln, at the head of whose corpse he had grimly sat as it rested from place to place on the triumphal progress to its burial, and from whose open grave he had hurried, in no very judicial humor to say the least, to take his seat among the Judges of the accused assassins. On his right sat Major-General Lew Wallace, a lawyer by profession; afterwards the President of the Court-Martial which tried and hung Henry Wirz; but now, by a sardonic freak of destiny, known to all the world as the tender teller of *Ben Hur, a Tale of the Christ*. To the right of General Wallace sat Brevet Brigadier-General James A. Ekin and Brevet Colonel Charles A. Tompkins; about whom the only thing remarkable is that they had stepped into the places of the two relieved officers, Colonel Tompkins being the only regular army officer on the Board. On the left of General Hunter sat, first, Brevet Major-General August V. Kautz, a native of Germany; next, Brigadier-General Robert S. Foster, who may or may not have been the "Colonel Foster" alluded to in the testimony of Lloyd quoted above, as threatening the witness and as afterwards being seen by him on the Commission – the presence of an officer, previously engaged by the Government in collecting testimony against the accused, as one of the judges to try him not being considered a violation of Military Justice. Next sat Brigadier-General Thomas Mealey Harris, a West Virginian, and the author of a book entitled

Calvinism Vindicated; next, Brigadier-General Albion P. Howe, and last, Lieutenant-Colonel David R. Clendenin.

Not one of these nine men could have withstood the challenge which the common law mercifully puts into the hands of the most abandoned culprit. They had come together with one determined and unchangeable purpose – to avenge the foul murder of their beloved Commander-in-Chief. They dreamt not of acquittal. They were, necessarily, from the very nature of their task, *organized to convict*.

The accused were asked, it is true, whether they had any objections to any member of the Court. But this was the emptiest of forms, as bias is no cause of challenge in military procedure, and peremptory challenges are unknown.

Moreover, it was nothing but a cruel mockery to offer to that trembling group of prisoners an opportunity, which, if any one of them had the temerity to embrace, could only have resulted in barbing with the sting of personal insult the hostile predisposition of the judges.

At the foot of the table around which the Court sat – the table standing parallel with the north side of the room – there was another, around which were gathered the three prosecuting officers, who, according to military procedure, were also members of the Commission.

First, was Brigadier-General Joseph Holt, the Judge-Advocate of the U.S. Army, and the Recorder of the Commission. During his past military career he had distinguished himself on many a bloody court-martial.

Second, designated by General Holt as First Assistant or Special Judge-Advocate, was Hon. John A. Bingham, of Ohio – long a Representative in Congress, then for a short interval a Military Judge-Advocate, now a Representative in Congress again, and to become in the strange vicissitudes of the near future, one of the managers of the impeachment of President Johnson, whom he now cannot praise too highly. He was one of those fierce and fiery western criminal lawyers, gifted with that sort of vociferous oratory which tells upon jurors and on the stump, by nature and training able to see but one side to a case and consequently merciless to his victims. His special function was to cross-examine and brow-beat the witnesses for the defense, a branch of his profession in which he was proudly proficient, and, above all, by pathetic appeals to their patriotism and loyalty, and by measureless denunciations of the murder of their Commander-in-Chief and of the Rebellion, to keep up at a white heat the already burning passions of the officers composing the tribunal. Next to him came Colonel Henry L. Burnett; brought from Indiana where he had won recent laurels in conducting the trial of Milligan for treason before a Military Commission – laurels, alas! soon to be blasted by the decision of the U.S. Supreme Court pronouncing that and all other Military Commissions for the trial of citizens in places where the civil courts are open illegal, and setting free the man this zealous public servant had been instrumental in condemning to death.

In the centre of the room was a witness-stand facing the Court. To the left of the witness-stand a table for the official reporters. Along the western side and directly opposite the Court was a platform about a foot high and four feet broad, with a strong railing in front of it. This was the prisoners' dock. The platform was divided near the left hand or southern corner by the doorway which led to the cells. In front of the southern end of the dock and behind the witness-stand was the table of the prisoners' counsel.

At the appointed hour the door in the western side opens and an impressive and mournful procession appears. Six soldiers armed to the teeth are interspersed among seven male prisoners and one woman.

First walks Samuel Arnold, the young Baltimorean, who is to sit at the extreme right (i.e., of the spectators), followed close by his armed guard; next, Dr. Samuel A. Mudd and a soldier; next, Edward Spangler and a soldier; next, Michael O'Laughlin, another Baltimorean, and his soldier; next, George B. Atzerodt and a soldier; next, Lewis Payne, a tall gladiator, though only twenty years old, and his soldier; and then David E. Herold, looking like an insignificant boy, who is to sit next the door. As they enter, their fetters clanking at every step, they turn to their left and take seats on the platform in the order named, the six soldiers being sandwiched here and there between two of the men.

Each of these prisoners, during the entire trial, was loaded down with irons made as massive and uncomfortable as possible. Their wrists were bound with the heaviest hand-cuffs, connected by bars of iron ten inches long (with the exception of Dr. Mudd, whose hand-cuffs were connected by a chain), so that they could not join their hands. Their legs were weighed down by shackles joined by chains made short enough to hamper their walk. In addition to these fetters, common to all, Payne and Atzerodt had, attached by chains to their legs, huge iron balls, which their guards had to lift and carry after them whenever they entered or left the Court room.

Last, there emerges from the dungeon-like darkness of the doorway the single female prisoner, Mary E. Surratt. She, alone, turns to her right and, consequently, when she is seated has the left hand corner of the platform to herself. But she is separated from her companions in misery by more than the narrow passageway that divides the dock; for she is a lady of fair social position, of unblemished character and of exemplary piety, and, besides, she is a mother, a widow, and, in that room amongst all those soldiers, lawyers, guards, judges and prisoners, the sole representative of her sex. Her womanhood is her peculiar weakness, yet still her only shield.

Is she too ironed?

The unanimous testimony of eye-witnesses published at the time of the trial is, that, though not hand-cuffed, she was bound with iron "anklets" on her feet. And this detail, thus universally proclaimed in the Northern Press and by loyal writers, was mentioned not as conveying the slightest hint of reprobation, but as constituting, like the case of the male prisoners, a part of the appropriate treatment by the military of a person suffering under such a charge. And, moreover, no contemporaneous denial of this widespread circumstance was anywhere made, either by Provost-Marshal, Counsel, Judge-Advocate or member of the Court. It passed unchallenged into history, like many another deed of shame, over which it is a wonder that any man could glory, but which characterized that period of frenzy.

Eight years after, during the bitter controversy between Andrew Johnson and Joseph Holt over the recommendation of mercy to Mrs. Surratt, General Hartranft, the former Special Provost-Marshal in charge of the prisoners, first broke silence and, coming to the aid of the sorely-tried Ex-Judge-Advocate, sent him a vehement categorical denial that Mrs. Surratt was ever manacled at any time, or that there was ever a thought of manacling her in any one's mind. Now, what force should be given to such a denial by so distinguished an officer, so long delayed and in the face of such universal contemporaneous affirmation?

No one knows how close and exclusive the charge of the prisoners by the special Provost-Marshal was, nor how liable to interruption, interference and supersession by the omnipotent Bureau of Military Justice, or by the maddened Secretary of War and his obsequious henchmen.

At the time the naked assertion was made, to heap indignities upon the head of the only woman in the whole country whom the soldiery took for granted was the one female fiend who helped to shed the blood of the martyred President, was so consonant with the angry feeling, in military circles, that an officer, having only a general superintendence over the custody and treatment of what was called "a band of fiends," would be very likely to overlook such a small matter as that the she-assassin was not exempted, in one detail, from the contumelies and cruelties it was thought patriotic to pile upon her co-conspirators. The only wonder ought to be that they relieved her from the hand-cuffs. They appear to have discriminated in the case of Dr. Mudd also, substituting a chain for an inflexible bar so that he for one could move his hands. There may have been some unmentioned physical reasons for both of these alleviations, but we may rest assured that neither sex, in the one case, nor profession in the other, was among them.

General Hartranft (or any other General) never denied, or

thought it necessary to deny, that the seven male prisoners sat through the seven weeks of the trial, loaded, nay tortured, with irons. And there is no doubt that this unspeakable outrage, if thought of at all at the trial by the soldiery – high or low – so far from being thought of as a matter of reprobation, was a subject of grim merriment or stern congratulation.

Eight years, however, passed away – eight years, in which a fund of indignation at such brutality, above all to a woman, had been silently accumulating, until at length to a soldier, whose beclouding passions of the moment had in the meantime cooled down, its weight made every loop-hole of escape an entrance for the very breath of life.

The entire atmosphere had changed, and denials became the order of the day. Memory is a most convenient faculty; and to forget what the lapse of years has at last stamped with infamy is easy, when the event passed at the time as a mere matter of course. Leaving these tardy repudiators of an iniquity, the responsibility for which in the day of its first publication they tacitly assumed with the utmost complacency, to settle the question with posterity – we insist that the preference is open to writers upon the events of the year 1865 to rely upon the unprejudiced and unchallenged statements of eye-witnesses; and, therefore, we do here reaffirm that Mary E. Surratt walked into the court-room, and sat during her trial, with shackles upon her limbs.

At this late day it is a most natural supposition that these nine stalwart military heroes, sitting comfortably around their table, arrayed in their bright uniforms, with their own arms and their own legs unfettered, must have felt at least a faint flush of mingled pity, shame and indignation, as they looked across that room at that ironed row of human beings.

Culprits arraigned before them, guarded by armed soldiery, without arms themselves – why, in the name of justice, drag them into Court and force them to sit through a long trial, bound with iron, hand and foot? Was it to forestall a last possible effort of reckless and suicidal despair?

These brave warriors could not have feared the naked arm

of Payne, nor have indulged the childish apprehension that seven unarmed men and one unarmed woman might overpower six armed soldiers and nine gallant officers, and effect their escape from the third story of a prison guarded on all sides with bayonets and watched by detective police! And yet, so far as appears, no single member of the Court, to whom such a desecration of our common humanity was a daily sight for weeks, thought it deserving of notice, much less of protest.

There is but one explanation of this moral insensibility, and that applies with the same force to the case of the woman as to those of the men. It is, that the accused were *already doomed*. For them no humiliation could be thought too deep, no indignity too vile, no hardship too severe, because their guilt was predetermined to be clear. And the members of the Military Commission, as they looked across the room at that sorry sight, saw nothing incongruous with justice, or even with the most chivalrous decorum, that the traitorous murderers of their beloved Commander-in-Chief should wear the shackles which were the proper precursors of the death of ignominy, they were resolved the outlaws should not escape.

We, civilians, must ever humbly bear in mind that the rule of the common law, that every person accused of crime is presumed to be innocent until his guilt is established beyond a reasonable doubt – a rule the benignity of which is often sneered at by soldiers as giving occasion for lawyers' tricks and quibbles, and as an impediment to swift justice, is reversed in military courts, where every person accused of crime is presumed to be *guilty* until he himself prove his innocence.

After the prisoners had been seated, and the members of the Commission, the Judge-Advocates and the official reporters sworn in, the accused were severally arraigned. There was but one Charge against the whole eight. Carefully formulated by the three Judge-Advocates upon the lines of the theory adopted by the Secretary of War, and which Gen. Baker and the Bureau of Military Justice had been moving heaven and earth to establish, it was so contrived as to allege a crime of such unprecedented, far-reaching and profound heinousness as to be an adequate cause of such an unprecedented and profound calamity.

The eight prisoners were jointly and severally charged with nothing less than having, in aid of the Rebellion, *"traitorously"* conspired, "together with one John H. Surratt, John Wilkes Booth, Jefferson Davis, George N. Sanders, Beverley Tucker, Jacob Thompson, William C. Cleary, Clement C. Clay, George Harper, George Young and others unknown, to kill and murder" "Abraham Lincoln, late President of the United States and Commander-in-Chief of the Army and Navy thereof, Andrew Johnson, then Vice-President, Wm. H. Seward, Secretary of State, and Ulysses S. Grant, Lieutenant-General;" and of having, in pursuance of such "traitorous conspiracy," "together with John Wilkes Booth and John H. Surratt" "traitorously" murdered Abraham Lincoln, "traitorously" assaulted with intent to kill, William H. Seward, and lain in wait "traitorously" to murder Andrew Johnson and Ulysses S. Grant.

On this elastic comprehensive Charge, in which treason and murder are vaguely commingled, every one of the men, and Mary E. Surratt, were arraigned, plead not guilty, and were put upon trial. There is no doubt, by the way, that the Secretary of War would have been included as one of the contemplated victims, had not Edwin M. Stanton borne so prominent a part in the prosecution; and it was for this reason, and not because of any change in the evidence, that General Grant stood alone, as the mark of O'Laughlin.

To this single Charge there was, also, but a single Specification. This document alleged that the design of all these traitorous conspirators was, to deprive the Army and Navy of their Commander-in-Chief and the armies of their Commander; to prevent a lawful election of President and Vice-President; and by such means to aid and comfort the Rebellion and overthrow the Constitution and laws.

It then alleged the killing of Abraham Lincoln by Booth in the prosecution of the conspiracy, and charged the murder to be the act of the prisoners, as well as of Booth and John H. Surratt.

It then alleged that Spangler, in furtherance of the conspiracy, aided Booth in obtaining entrance to the box of the theatre, in barring the door of the theatre box, and in effecting his escape. Then, that Herold, in furtherance of the conspiracy, aided and abetted Booth in the murder, and in effecting his escape. Then, that Payne, in like furtherance, made the murderous assault on Seward and also on his two sons and two attendants. Then, that Atzerodt, in like furtherance, at the same hour of the night, lay in wait for Andrew Johnson with intent to kill him. Then, that Michael O'Laughlin, in like furtherance, on the nights of the 13th and 14th of April, lay in wait for General Grant with like intent. Then, that Samuel Arnold, in prosecution of the conspiracy, "did, on or before the 6th day of March, 1865, and on divers other days and times between that day and the 15th day of April, 1865, combine, conspire with and counsel, abet, comfort and support" Booth, Payne, Atzerodt, O'Laughlin and their confederates. Then, "that, in prosecution of the conspiracy, Mary E. Surratt, on or before the 6th of March, 1865, and on divers other days and times between that day and the 20th of April, 1865, received, entertained, harbored and concealed, aided and assisted" Booth, Herold, Payne, John H. Surratt, O'Laughlin, Atzerodt, Arnold and their confederates, "with the knowledge of the murderous and traitorous conspiracy aforesaid, and with intent to aid, abet and assist them in the execution thereof, and in escaping from justice." And, lastly, that in prosecution of the conspiracy Samuel A. Mudd did from on or before the 6th day of March, to the 20th of April "advise, encourage, receive, entertain, harbor and conceal, aid and assist" Booth, Herold, Payne, John H. Surratt, O'Laughlin, Atzerodt, Mary E. Surratt, Arnold and their confederates, in its execution and their escape.

After the prisoners, who as yet had no counsel, had pleaded not guilty to the Charge and Specification, the Court adopted rules of proceeding – one of which was that the sessions of the Court should be secret, and no one but the sworn officers and the counsel for the prisoners, also sworn to secrecy, should be admitted, except by permit of the President of the Commission; and that only such portions of the testimony as the Judge-Advocate should designate should be made public.

On the next day (Thursday, May 11th), Mr. Thomas Ewing, Jr. and Mr. Frederick Stone appeared as counsel for Dr. Mudd, and Mr. Frederick A. Aiken and Mr. John W. Clampitt for Mrs. Surratt; and on the succeeding day (12th), Mr. Frederick Stone appeared for Herold "at the earnest request of his widowed mother and estimable sisters;" General Ewing for Arnold (and on Monday, the 15th, for Spangler); Mr. Walter S. Cox for O'Laughlin, and Mr. William E. Doster for Payne and Atzerodt.

By the rules of the Commission no counsel could appear for the prisoners unless he took the "iron-clad oath" or filed evidence of having taken it. So supersensitive was the loyalty of the Court that it could not brook the presence of a "sympathizer with the South," even in such a confidential relation as counsel for accused conspirators in aid of the Rebellion.

The demeanor of the Court towards the counsel for the defense, reflecting as in a mirror the humor of the Judge-Advocates, was highly characteristic. Sometimes they were treated with haughty indifference, sometimes with ironical condescension, often with contumely, generally with contempt. Their objections were invariably overruled, unless acceded to by the Judge-Advocate. The Commission could not conceal its secret opinion that they were engaged in a disreputable and disloyal employment.

This statement must be somewhat qualified, however, so far as it relates to General Ewing. He was, or had been recently, of equal rank in the army of the Union with the members of the Court. He was a brother-in-law of General Sherman, and he had acquired a high reputation for gallantry and skill, as well as loyalty, during the war. That such a distinguished fellow-soldier should appear to defend the fiendish murderers of their beloved Commander-in-Chief – outlaws they were detailed as a Court to hang – evidently perplexed and disconcerted these military Judges and tended in some degree to curb the over-bearing insolence of the Special Judge-Advocate. Thus, this able lawyer and gallant officer and noble man was enabled to be "the leading spirit of the defense;" and, as we shall see, he wrought the miracle of plucking from the deadly clutches of the Judge-Advocates the lives of every one of the men he defended. But this instance was a most notable exception. As a rule, even the silent presence of the counsel for the accused jarred upon the feelings of the Court, and their vocal interference provoked, at intervals, its outspoken animadversion. A trifling incident will serve to illustrate.

The witnesses, while giving their testimony, were required to face the Court, so that they necessarily turned their backs on the counsel for the prisoners who were placed some distance behind the witness-stand. These counsel were also forced to cross-examine the witnesses for the prosecution, and interrogate their own, without seeing their faces; and as often as a witness in instinctive obedience to the dictates of good manners would turn round to answer a question, the President of the Court would check him by a "sharp reprimand" and the stern admonition: "Face the Court!" The confusion of a witness, especially for the defense, when thundered at in this way by General Hunter, and the reiterated humiliation of counsel implied in the order, seem to have only called forth the wonder that witnesses "would persist in turning towards the prisoners' counsel!"

Clearly these lawyers were an unmeaning, an impeding, an offensive, though unavoidable, superfluity.

CHAPTER FOUR
Animus of the Judges

On Saturday, the 13th of May, an incident occurred which throws much light upon the judicial temper of the Court at the very beginning of the trial. On that day Reverdy Johnson appeared as counsel for Mrs. Surratt. Admitted to the bar in 1815, Senator of the United States as far back as 1845, Attorney-General of the United States as long ago as 1849, and holding the position of Senator of the United States again at that very moment; having taken the constitutional oath in all the Courts including the Supreme Court of the United States at whose bar he was one of the most eminent advocates; three years after this time to be Minister Plenipotentiary to England; as he stood there, venerable both in years and in honors, appearing at great personal and professional sacrifice, gratuitously, for a woman in peril of her life, one would have thought him secure at least from insult. Yet no sooner did he announce his intention, if the Court would permit him at any time to attend to his imperative duties elsewhere, to act as counsel, than the President of the Commission read aloud a note he had received from one of his colleagues objecting "to the admission of Reverdy Johnson as a counsel before this Court on the ground that he does not recognize the moral obligation of an oath that is designed as a test of loyalty;" and, in support of the objection, referring to Mr. Johnson's letter to the people of Maryland pending the adoption of the new constitution of 1864.

The following colloquy then took place:

> Mr. Johnson: May I ask who the member of the Court is that makes that objection?
> The President: Yes, sir, it is General Harris, and, if he had not made it, I should have made it myself.
> Mr. Johnson: I do not object to it at all. The Court will decide if I am to be tried.
> The President: The Court will be cleared.
> Mr. Johnson: I hope I shall be heard.
> General Ekin: I think it can be decided without clearing the Court.
> General Wallace: I move that Mr. Johnson be heard.
> The President and others: Certainly.
> Mr. Johnson: Is the opinion here to which the objection refers?
> The President: I think it is not.

It was discovered, farther on, that General Harris by his own admissions had not even seen the opinion since he had read it a year ago, and that his objection, involving so grave an attack upon the moral character of so distinguished a man, was based upon a mere recollection of its contents after that lapse of time.

Naturally, the gray-haired statesman and lawyer was indignant at this premeditated insult. In his address to the Court he repudiated with scorn the interpretation put upon his letter by his accuser. He explained the circumstances under which the opinion was delivered; that the Maryland Convention had prescribed an oath to the voter which they had no right to exact; "and all that the opinion said, or was intended to say, was, that to take the oath voluntarily was not a craven submission to usurped authority, but was necessary in order to enable the citizen to protect his rights under the then constitution; and that there was no moral harm in taking an oath which the Convention had no authority to impose."

Among other things he said:

There is no member of this Court, including the President, and the member that objects, who recognizes the obligation of an oath more absolutely than I do; and there is nothing in my life, from its commencement to the present time, which would induce me for a moment to avoid a comparison in all moral respects between myself and any member of this Court.

If such an objection was made in the Senate of the United States, where I am known, I forbear to say how it would be treated.

I have lived too long, gone through too many trials, rendered the country such services as my abilities enabled me, and the confidence of the people in whose midst I am has given me the opportunity, to tolerate for a moment – come from whom it may – such an aspersion upon my moral character. I am glad it is made now, when I have arrived at that period of life when it would be unfit to notice it in any other way.

I am here at the instance of that lady (pointing to Mrs. Surratt) whom I never saw until yesterday, and never heard of, she being a Maryland lady; and thinking that I could be of service to her, and protesting as she has done her innocence to me – of the facts I know nothing – because I deemed it right, I deemed it due to the character of the profession to which I belong, and which is not inferior to the noble profession of which you are members, that she should not go undefended. I knew I was to do it voluntarily, without compensation; the law prohibits me from receiving compensation; but if it did not, understanding her condition, I should never have dreamed of refusing upon the ground of her inability to make compensation.

General Harris, in reply, insisted that the remarks of Mr. Johnson, explanatory of the letter, corroborated his construction.

I understand him to say that the doctrine which he taught the people of his state was, that because the Convention had framed an oath, which was unconstitutional and illegal in his opinion, therefore it had no moral binding force, and that people might take it and then go and vote without any regard to the subject matter, of the oath.

Mr. Johnson, interrupting, denied having said any such thing. General Hunter, thereupon, to help his colleague out, had the remarks read from the record. Mr. Johnson assenting to the correctness of the report, General Harris continued: "If that language does not justify my conclusion, I confess I am unable to understand the English language;" and then repeated his construction of the letter.

After he had concluded, Mr. Johnson endeavored to show the author of *Calvinism Vindicated* that he did not understand the English language, by pointing out the distinction between stating "there was no harm in taking an oath, and telling the people of Maryland that there would be no harm in breaking it after it was taken." Again repelling the misconstruction attempted to be put upon his words, he proceeded to open a new line as follows:

> But, as a legal question, it is something new to me that the objection, if it was well founded in fact is well founded in law. Who gives to the Court the jurisdiction to decide upon the moral character of the counsel who may appear before them? Who makes them the arbiters of the public morality and professional morality? What authority have they, under their commission, to rule me out, or to rule any other counsel out, upon the ground, above all, that he does not recognize the validity of an oath, even if they believed it?

General Harris, in rejoinder, stated that under the rules adopted by the Commission gentlemen appearing as counsel for the accused must either produce a certificate of having taken the oath of loyalty or take it before the Court, and that therefore the Court had a right to inquire whether counsel held such opinions as to be incompetent to take the oath. He then expressed his gladness "to give the gentleman the benefit of his disclaimer. It is satisfactory to me, but it is, I must insist, a tacit admission that there was some ground for the view upon which my objection was founded."

Mr. Johnson closed this irritating discussion by saying:

> The order under which you are assembled gives you no

authority to refuse me admission because you have no authority to administer the oath to me. I have taken the oath in the Senate of the United States – the very oath that you are administering; I have taken it in the Circuit Court of the United States; I have taken it in the Supreme Court of the United States; and I am a practitioner in all the Courts of the United States in nearly all the States; and it would be a little singular if one who has a right to appear before the supreme judicial tribunal of the land, and who has a right to appear before one of the Legislative departments of the Government whose law creates armies, and creates judges and courts-martial, should not have a right to appear before a court-martial. I have said all that I proposed to say.

The President of the Court, who had already made himself a party to this gross insult to a distinguished counsel – as if disappointed that the affair was about to end so smoothly – here burst out:

> Mr. Johnson has made an intimation in regard to holding members of this Court personally responsible for their action.
> Mr. Johnson: I made no such intimation; did not intend it.
> The President: Then I shall say nothing more, sir.
> Mr. Johnson: I had no idea of it. I said I was too old to feel such things, if I even would.
> The President: I was going to say that I hoped the day had passed when freemen from the North were to be bullied and insulted by the humbug chivalry; and that, for my own part, I hold myself personally responsible for everything I do here. The Court will be cleared.

On reopening, the Judge-Advocate read a paper from General Harris withdrawing his objection because of Mr. Johnson's disclaimer. General Wallace remarked that it must be known to every member of the Commission that Mr. Senator Johnson had taken the oath in the Senate of the United States. He therefore suggested that the requirement of his taking the oath be dispensed with.

The suggestion was acquiesced in, *nem. con.*
Mr. Johnson: I appear, then, as counsel for Mrs. Surratt.

In reviewing, at this distance of time, the foregoing scene, it is scarcely possible to realize the state of mind of a member of a tribunal claiming at least to be a court of justice, that could prompt such an onslaught – so shocking to the universal expectation of dignity and decorum, not to say absolute impartiality, in a judge.

The interpretation put upon the letter of Reverdy Johnson to his constituents by Generals Harris and Hunter was the ordinary, ill-considered, second-hand version circulated by blind party hostility. This is clearly shown by the fact that the objection of General Harris was not founded upon a recent perusal of the letter, but upon his own recollection of the impression it made in his own party circles the year before.

When, on the next Wednesday, General Harris, having in the meantime looked it up, presented a copy of the incriminated opinion, prefacing a request that it be made a part of the record by the sneering remark that "the Honorable gentleman ought to be very thankful to me for having made an occasion for him to disclaim before the country any obliquity of intention in writing that letter;" and, on the suggestion of General Hunter, the letter was read; every fair minded man ought to have been convinced that it was open to such a malign misconstruction only by an unscrupulous political enemy.

But suppose for a moment that their own hasty and uncharitable construction was correct, what right – what color of justification – did that give these two military Judges to make that letter of the year before the pretext for a sudden attack in open court upon such a man as Reverdy Johnson, and on the consecrated occasion of his appearing as counsel for a lady on trial for her life?

As to General Harris' argument that the requirement of an oath gave the Commission a right to inquire whether the written opinions of a counsel chosen for a defendant, previously delivered as a party leader, were of such a character as to render him incompetent to take an oath which the Supreme Court of the United States and the Senate of the United States had recognized his competency to take; why, it is charitable to suppose – and his subsequent claim would have been scouted as preposterous in any law-court in the world.

With regard to General Hunter, his ferocious personal defiance, hurled from the very Bench, demonstrated in a flash his preëminent unfitness for any function that is judicial even in a military sense. It is manifest that this whole attack, whether concerted or not, was not made from any conscientious regard for the sanctity of an oath, nor from any sensitive fear that Reverdy Johnson, as an oath-breaker, might contaminate the tribunal; but it was either a mere empty ebullition of party spleen, or of party hatred towards a distinguished democrat, or it was made with a deliberate design to rob a poor woman of any probable advantage such eminent counsel might procure for her.

And whether the latter terrible suspicion be well founded or not, true it is that this cruel result, notwithstanding the withdrawal of the objection, did not fail of full accomplishment.

Reverdy Johnson, though suffered to appear as counsel, was virtually out of the case. He was present only at rare intervals during the trial, and sent in his final argument to be read by one of his juniors. The Court had put its brand upon him, and to any subsequent effort of his it turned an indifferent countenance and a deaf ear. He, forsooth, had "sympathized" with the Rebellion and that was enough! His appearance worked only harm to his client, if harm could be done to one whom the Court believed to have been also a sympathizer with rebellion, and who was already doomed to suffer in the place of her uncaptured son.

Another incident, occurring after the testimony on behalf of the prisoners had begun, will illustrate still more clearly, if possible, the mental attitude of the Court.

Among the witnesses sworn on the first day of the trial in secret session was one Von Steinacker, who, according to his own statement, had been in the Confederate Army, on the staff of

Major-General Edward Johnson. He told the usual cock-and-bull story about seeing Booth in Virginia, in 1863, consorting with the rebel officers and concocting the assassination of Lincoln. At the time of his examination he was a prisoner of war, but after he had given his testimony he was discharged. The counsel for the defense knowing nothing of the witness did not cross-examine him at all. But, subsequently, they discovered that, after having once been convicted of an attempt to desert, he had at last succeeded in deserting the Union Army, and had entered the service of the Confederates; that he had been convicted of theft by a court-martial; and that his whole story was a fiction. Thereupon, as soon as possible, the counsel for Mrs. Surratt applied for the recall of the witness for cross-examination, so as to lay the basis for his contradiction and impeachment; and they embodied the facts they were ready to prove in a paper which was signed by Reverdy Johnson and the other counsel for Mrs. Surratt. This application seems to have strangely disturbed the Judge-Advocates and aroused the ire of the Court. The prosecuting officers professed to have no knowledge of the whereabouts of the witness; and General Wallace, moved from his wonted propriety, delivered himself as follows:

> I, for my part, object to the appearance of any such paper on the record, and wish to say now that I understand distinctly and hold in supreme contempt, such practices as this. It is very discreditable to the parties concerned, to the attorneys, and, if permitted, in my judgment will be discreditable to the Court.

Mr. Clampitt, with the most obsequious deference to the Court, deprecated any such reflection upon the conduct of counsel and alluded to their duty to their unfortunate clients. But this humble apology was declared not satisfactory to the General or to the Court; and the application was not only refused but the paper was not allowed to go upon the record. However, this summary method of keeping facts out of sight availed nothing. Mrs. Surratt's counsel had caused to be summoned as a witness, to contradict and impeach Von Steinacker, Edward Johnson, the very Major-General on whose staff the witness had sworn he had been.

General Johnson, a distinguished officer in the Confederate Army, was taken prisoner in 1864 and had been in confinement since, as such, at Fort Warren. From thence he had been brought to attend before the Commission in obedience to a subpœna issued by the Court.

On the 30th of May, he was called as a witness and appeared upon the stand to be sworn. As he stood there, in his faded uniform, bearing, doubtless, traces of the six months' imprisonment from which he had come at the command of the Court, facing the officers of the Army he had so often encountered, and with his back turned upon the woman on whose behalf he had been summoned; General Albion P. Howe deemed it his duty as an impartial judge to make the following attack upon him.

After stating that it was well known that "the person" before the Court had been educated at the National Military Academy, and had since for many years held a commission in the U.S. Army, and had therefore taken the oath of allegiance, this gallant officer and upright judge proceeded:

> In 1861, it became my duty as an officer to fire upon a rebel party, of which this man was a member, and that party fired upon, struck down, and killed loyal men that were in the service of the Government. I understand that he is brought here now as a witness to testify before this Court, and he comes here as a witness with his hands red with the blood of his loyal countrymen, shed by him or by his assistants, in violation of his solemn oath as a man and his faith as an officer. I submit to this Court that he stands in the eye of the law as an incompetent witness, because he is notoriously infamous. To offer as a witness a man who stands with this character, who has openly violated the obligations of his oath, and his faith as an officer, and to administer the oath to him and present his testimony, is but an insult to the Court and an outrage upon the administration of justice. I move that this man, Edward Johnson, be ejected from the Court as an incompetent witness on account of his notorious infamy on the grounds I have

stated.

General Ekin welcomed the opportunity to distinguish himself by seconding the motion and characterizing the appearance of the witness before the Commission, "with such a character" as "the height of impertinence!" In his haste to insult a fallen foe, he seems to have forgotten that the witness had no alternative but to come.

The counsel for the prisoner humbly reminded the Court that the prosecution itself had sworn as its own witnesses men who had borne arms against the Government. The Judge-Advocate saw that the members of the Court had gone too far, and, after calling their attention to the familiar rule that the record of conviction in a judicial proceeding was the only basis of a total rejection of a witness, proceeded to provide a channel for the relief of the Court by suggesting that they could discredit the witness upon the ground stated, although they could not declare him incompetent to testify.

The assertion is confidently made that in the whole annals of English criminal jurisprudence, full as they are of instances of the grossest unfairness to persons on trial, no such outrage upon the administration of justice as the foregoing can be found. To find its parallel you must go to the records of the French Revolutionary Tribunal. What are we to think of the complaint of a Union General, that "a rebel party" fired (first? No! but that when "it became his duty as an officer to fire upon a rebel party" the rebel party fired) back? What in Mars' name did this warrior expect? Would he have had kinder feelings towards his brave adversary if, in response to his own volley, the Confederate General had tamely laid down his arms, or played the coward and run?

Nowadays, when the blue and the gray meet, charges of infamy are no longer heard, but the more deadly the past warfare, the greater the reciprocal respect.

However, this unprovoked assault upon an unoffending officer, powerless to repel it, although it did not result in his ejection from the Court, effectually disposed of General Johnson as a witness.

In answer to the questions of counsel he calmly gave his testimony, which exploded both Von-Steinacker and his story. Judge Bingham confined his cross-examination to eliciting the facts, that the witness had graduated from West Point, served in the U.S. Army until 1861, resigned, and joined the Confederate Army. The Court paid no attention to his direct testimony because he had fired upon Union men when they had fired upon him.

The foregoing incidents conclusively show (were any such demonstration necessary) that a Board of nine military officers, fresh from service in the field in a bloody civil war, with all the fierce prejudices naturally bred by such a conflict hot within their bosoms, was the most unfit tribunal possible to administer impartial justice to eight persons charged with the murder of the Commander-in-Chief of the Army to which every member of the Court belonged, committed in aid of that Rebellion which during four years of hard fighting they had helped to suppress.

CHAPTER FIVE
The Conduct of the Trial

  The whole conduct of the trial emphasizes this conclusion. The Court, in weighing the evidence, adopted and acted upon the following proposition; that any witness, sworn for any of the prisoners, who had enlisted in the Confederate service, or had at any time expressed secession sentiments, or sympathized in any way with the South, was totally unworthy of credit. The Court went a step farther, and adopted the monstrous rule that participation in the Rebellion was evidence of participation in the assassination! This assertion now seems incredible, but it is fully attested by the record. At one stage of the trial, the Judge-Advocate asked a witness whether or not the prisoner Arnold had been in the military service of the rebels. General Ewing, his counsel, strenuously objected to this question on the ground, that it tended to prove the prisoner guilty of another crime than the one for which he was on trial, and thus to prejudice him in the eyes of the Court.

  Judge Holt remarked:

> How kindred to each other are the crimes of treason against a nation and assassination of its chief magistrate.
>
> The murder of the President... was preëminently a political assassination.
>
> When, therefore, we shall show, on the part of the ac-

cused, acts of intense disloyalty, bearing arms in the field against the Government, we show with him the presence of an animus towards the Government which relieves this accusation of much, if not all, of its improbability.

He asserted that such a course of proof was constantly resorted to in criminal courts; and when General Ewing challenged him (as well he might) to produce any authorities for such a position, he called upon the indomitable Bingham to state them.

The Special Judge-Advocate responded, but he courteously, but unmistakably, shied away from his colleague's position and put the competency of the testimony upon another ground, viz.: that where the intent with which a thing was done is in issue, other acts of the prisoner which tend to prove the intent may be given in evidence. Here he was dealing with a familiar principle, and could cite any number of cases. He then proceeded to apply his good law. How? By claiming that conspiracy to murder having been laid in the charge, "*with the intent to aid the Rebellion,*" that was the intent in issue here, and therefore to prove that a man was in the Rebellion went to prove that intent.

At the request of General Ewing he read the allegation which ran "in aid of the Rebellion," and not "*with intent* to aid," and the counsel pointed out that that was "an allegation of fact, and not of intent;" but the Judge insisted that it was in effect an allegation of intent – implied if not expressed.

General Ewing then replied to his adversary's argument by showing that such an allegation was an unnecessary allegation. Conspiracy to murder and attempted murder were crimes done with *intent to kill*; and it was a matter of no moment in pleading to allege a general intent to aid the Rebellion. Courts had no right to violate the laws of evidence because the prosecution has seen fit to violate the laws of pleading.

Judge Bingham contended (and cited authorities) for his familiar law, and then again in applying it triumphantly asked, "When he [Arnold] entered it (i.e., the Rebellion) he entered into it to aid it, did he not?"

Mr. Ewing replied, "He did not enter into that to assassinate the President."

At this, the Assistant Judge-Advocate rising to the decisive and culminating point of his argument gave utterance to the following proposition:

> Yes: he entered into it to assassinate the President; and everybody else that entered into the Rebellion entered into it to assassinate everybody that represented the Government, that either followed the standard in the field, or represented its standard in the counsels. That is exactly why it is germane.

And, thereupon, the Commission immediately overruled the objection. General Ewing told the exact truth, without a particle of rhetorical exaggeration, when, in the closing sentence of his argument against the jurisdiction of the Commission, he exclaimed:

> Indeed, the position taken by the learned Assistant Judge-Advocate... goes to this – and even beyond it – namely, that participation in the Rebellion was participation in the assassination, and that the Rebellion itself formed part of the conspiracy for which these men are on trial here.

Throughout the whole trial, the Commission took the law from the Judge-Advocates with the unquestioning docility usually manifested by a jury on such matters in civil courts. In truth, the main function of a Judge-Advocate appears to be to furnish law to the Court, as in civil courts the main function of the Judge is to furnish law to the jury. Consequently, his exposition of the law on any disputed point – whether relative to modes of procedure, or to the competency of testimony, or even to questions of jurisdiction – instead of standing on the same level with the antagonistic exposition of counsel for the accused as an argument to be weighed by the Court against its opposite in the equal scales of decision, was at all times authoritative, like the opinion of a judge overruling the contention of a lawyer. This, surely, was bad enough for a defendant; but, what was still more fatal to his chances of fair dealing, this habit of domination, acquiesced in by the Court on questions of law, had the effect (as is also seen in civil courts) of giving the same superior force to the expositions of questions of fact by the Judge-Advocate. And as this office combined the functions of a prosecuting officer with the functions of a judge, there could be no restraints of law, custom or personal delicacy, against the enforcement, with all the powers of reasoning and appeal at command, the conclusion of the Judge-Advocate upon the matters of fact.

In a word, the judgment of the prosecuting officer – the retained counsel for the Government, the plaintiff in the action – ruled with absolute sway, both on the law and on the facts, the judgment of the Commission; the members of which, for that matter, were also in the pay of the Government.

It may, therefore, be readily anticipated with how little impartiality the trial was conducted.

Mrs. Surratt (as did the rest of the accused) plead to the jurisdiction of the Commission on the grounds (1) that she was not and had not been in the military service of the United States, and (2) that when the crimes charged were committed the civil courts were open in Washington; both of which allegations were admitted and were notoriously true. Whatever might be the indifference with which the rights of the men to a constitutional trial may have been viewed, it was so utterly incongruous with the spirit of military jurisprudence and so unprecedented in practice to try a woman by court-martial, that had Mrs. Surratt been alone before that Commission we venture to say those nine soldiers could not have brought themselves, or allowed the Judge-Advocate to bring them, to the overruling of her plea. As it was, however, the court-room was cleared of all save the members of the Commission and the three Judge-Advocates; and after a season of what is called "deliberation" (which meant the further enforcement of the opinion of the prosecuting officers upon the point under discussion, where necessary), the court reopened and "the Judge-Advocate announced that the pleas... had been overruled by the

Commission."

Mrs. Surratt (as did the other prisoners) then asked for a separate trial; a right guaranteed to her in all the civil courts of the vicinage. It was denied to her, without discussion, as a matter of course.

And yet no one now can fail to recognize the grievous disadvantage under which this one woman labored, coupled in a single trial with such culprits as Payne who confessed his guilt, and Herold who was captured with Booth.

In fact, the scheme of trial contrived by the Judge-Advocates on a scale comprehensive enough to embrace the prisoners, the Canadian exiles and the Confederate Cabinet, would not work on a trial of Mrs. Surratt alone. Of this pet plan they were highly proud and greatly enamoured. To it, everything – the rights of woman as well as man; considerations of equity and of common fairness – must be made to give way.

To the maintenance of this scheme in its integrity, they had marshalled the witnesses, and they guided the Commission with a firm hand so that not a jot or tittle of its symmetry should be marred.

This determined purpose is indicated by the starting-point they chose for the testimony.

On Friday, the twelfth, the first witness was sworn, and his name was Richard Montgomery. His testimony, as well as that of the other witnesses sworn that day, was taken in secret session, and no portion of it was allowed to reach the public until long after the trial. It was all directed to establish the complicity of the rebel agents in Canada and through them the complicity of Jefferson Davis and other officers of the "Confederacy" in the assassination. In other words, this testimony was given to prove the guilt, not of the men much less of the woman on trial, but of the men included in the charge but not on trial; and whom, as it now appears, the United States never intended to try.

To connect the defunct Confederacy in the person of its captive Chief with the murder of the President would throw a halo of romantic wickedness about the crime, and chime in with the prevalent hatred towards every human being in any way connected with the Rebellion.

This class of testimony continued to be introduced every now and then during the trial – whenever most convenient to the prosecution – and as often as it was given the court-room was cleared of spectators and the session secret; the isolated counsel for Mrs. Surratt, utterly at a loss to imagine the connection of such testimony, given under such solemn precautions, with their own client, and knowing nothing whatever of the witnesses themselves, must have looked on in bewildered amazement, and had no motive for cross-examination.

The chief witnesses who gave this carefully suppressed evidence were spies upon the rebel agents in Canada paid by the United States, and, at the same time, spies upon the United States paid by the rebel agents.

They were, of course, ready to swear to as many conversations with these agents, both before and after the assassination, in which those agents implicated themselves and the heads of government at Richmond in the most reckless manner, as the Judge-Advocates thought necessary or advisable.

The head, parent and tutor of this band of witnesses was a man called Sanford Conover. After giving his testimony before the Commission, he went to Canada and again resumed his simulated intimacy with the Confederates there, passing under the name of James W. Wallace. An unauthorized version of his testimony having leaked out and appearing in the newspapers, he was called to account for it by his Canadian friends. He then made and published an affidavit that the person who had given testimony before the Commission was not himself but an imposter, and at the same time also published an offer of $500 reward for the arrest of "the infamous and perjured scoundrel who secretly personated me under name of Sanford Conover, and deposed to a tissue of falsehood before the military Commission at Washington."

Being reclaimed by the government from his Canadian perils, he appeared again before the Court after the testimony had been closed and the summing up of all the prisoners' counsel had been completed (June 27th); when he testified that his affidavit had been extorted from him by the Confederates in Canada by threats of death at the point of a pistol. This man Conover was subsequently (in 1867) tried and convicted of perjury and sent to the penitentiary; and with him the whole structure of perjured testimony, fabricated for reward by him and Montgomery and their co-spies, fell to the ground. Secretary Seward testified before the Judiciary Committee of the House of Representatives, in 1867, that, "the testimony of these witnesses was discredited and destroyed by transactions in which Sanford Conover appeared and the evidence of the alleged complicity of Jefferson Davis thereupon failed."

But, at the period of the trial, when the passionate desire for vengeance was at its height, any plausible scoundrel, whose livelihood depended on the rewards for wholesale perjury, and who was sure to be attracted to Washington by the scent of his favorite game, was thrice welcome to the Bureau of Military Justice. Any story, no matter how absurd or incredible, provided it brought Jefferson Davis within conjectural fore-knowledge of the assassination, was greedily swallowed, and, moreover, was rewarded with money and employment. These harpies flocked, like buzzards, around the doors of the old Penitentiary, and all – black and white, from Richmond, from Washington and from Montreal – were eager, for a consideration, to swear that Davis and Benjamin were the instigators of Booth and Surratt. And such testimony as it was! For the most part the sheerest hearsay! The private impressions of the witness! In one instance, his recollection of the contents of a letter the witness had heard read or talked about, the signature of which, although he did not see it himself, he heard was the signature of Jefferson Davis!! Testimony wholly inadmissible under the most elementary rules of evidence, but swept before the Commission in the absence of counsel for the parties implicated and under the immunity of a secret session.

For example: a blind man, who had been, at an undated period during the war, a hanger-on around the camp at Richmond, being asked whether he had heard any conversations among the rebel officers in regard to the contemplated assassination, answered:

> In a general way, I have heard sums offered, to be paid with a Confederate sum, for any person or persons to go North and assassinate the President.

Being pressed to name the amount and by what officers, he answered:

> At this moment, I cannot tell you the particular names of shoulder-straps, &c.
> Q: Do you remember any occasion – some dinner occasion?
> A: I can tell you this: I heard a citizen make the remark once, that he would give from his private purse $10,000, in addition to the Confederate amount, to have the President assassinated; to bring him to Richmond dead or alive, for proof.
> Q: I understood you to say that it was a subject of general conversation among the rebel officers?
> A: It was. The rebel officers, as they would be sitting around their tent doors, would be conversing on such a subject a great deal. They would be saying they would like to see his head brought there, dead or alive, and they should think it could be done; and I have heard such things stated as that they had certain persons undertaking it.

In the introduction of evidence against Mrs. Surratt, as well as the others on trial, the Judge-Advocates allowed themselves the most unlimited range.

Narrations of all sorts of events connected with the progress of the War – historical, problematical or fabulous – having no relevancy to the particular charge against her, or them, but deadly in their tendency to steel the minds of the Court against her, were admitted without scruple or hesitation.

Seven soldiers who had been prisoners of war at Libby Prison, Belle Island or Andersonville were called and testified, in all its ghastly details, to the terrible treatment they and their fellow-prisoners had undergone. Three witnesses were sworn to prove that the rebel government buried a torpedo under the centre of Libby Prison, to be fired if the U.S. troops entered Richmond. Letters found in the Richmond Archives were read, offering to rid the world of the Confederacy's deadliest enemies, and projecting wholesale destruction to property in the North. Testimony was allowed to be given of the burning of U.S. transports and bridges by men in the Confederate service; of the raids from Canada into the United States; of the alleged plot in all its horrible features to introduce the yellow-fever into Northern cities by infected clothing, testified to by the villain who swore he did it for money. It is scarcely to be credited, yet it is a fact, that the confession of Robert Kennedy, hung in March previous for attempting to burn the City of New York, was read in evidence; as was also a letter from a Confederate soldier, detailing the blowing up of vessels by a torpedo and the killing of Union men at City Point, indorsed by a recommendation of the operator to favor.

On June 27th, after the testimony had been closed and the summing up of counsel for the defense ended, the case was re-opened and there was introduced an advertisement clipped from the Selma *Dispatch* of December 1st, 1864, wherein some anonymous lunatic offered, if furnished $1,000,000, to cause the lives of Lincoln, Seward and Johnson to be taken before the first of March.

The prosecution closed its direct testimony on May 25th, reserving the right (of which we have seen they availed themselves from time to time) thereafter to call further witnesses on the character of the Rebellion and the complicity of its leaders in the assassination.

Out of about one hundred and fifty witnesses sixty-six gave testimony of that kind. Of the remaining eighty-four about fifty testified to the circumstances attending the assassination, the pursuit and capture of Booth and Herold, and the terrific assault of Payne on William H. Seward and his household. Of the remaining thirty-four there were nine whose testimony was directed to the incrimination of Mrs. Surratt.

The important witnesses against her were three soldiers testifying under the eye of their superior officers as to her non-recognition of Payne, and two informers who had turned state's evidence to save their own necks, who connected her with Booth.

The witnesses for the defense, for the most part, were treated by the Special Judge-Advocate as virtual accomplices of the accused; and, as soon as, by a searching cross-examination, he had extorted from them a reluctant admission of the slightest sympathy with the South (as in almost every case he was able to do), he swept them aside as impeached, and their testimony as unworthy of a moment's consideration. A former slave, who announced himself or herself as ready to give evidence against his or her former master, was a delicious morsel for the Bureau of Military Justice; and several such were sworn for the prosecution. While, on the other hand, nothing so exasperated the loyal Bingham or so astonished the Court as the apparition of an old slave-woman, summoned by the defense, eagerly endeavoring to exculpate her former master.

Several priests testified as to the good character of Mrs. Surratt as a lady and a Christian, but the effect of their testimony was immediately demolished in the eyes of the Court, when, on cross-examination, although they refused to substantiate what the Judge-Advocate called "her notorious intense disloyalty," they could not remember that they had ever heard her "utter one loyal sentiment."

CHAPTER SIX
Arguments For the Defense

The testimony for the several defenses of the eight accused closed on the 7th of June, and the testimony in rebuttal ended on the 14th, with the evidence of the physicians on the sanity of Payne.

Thereupon, General Ewing endeavored to extract from the Judge-Advocate an answer to the two following questions: First. Whether his clients were on trial for but one crime, viz.: Conspiracy, or four crimes, viz.: Conspiracy, Murder, Attempt at murder, Lying in wait? and

Second. By what statute or code of laws the crimes of "traitorously" murdering, or "traitorously" assaulting with intent to kill, or "traitorously" lying in wait, were defined, and what was the punishment affixed?

The Judge-Advocate's reply to the first question was, in substance, that all the accused were charged with conspiring to assassinate the President and the other members of the Government named, and further, with having executed that conspiracy so far as the assassination of the President and the assault on the Secretary of State were concerned, and "to have attempted its execution so far as concerns the lying in wait and other matters."

Assistant Judge-Advocate Bingham added:

The act of any one of the parties to a conspiracy in its execution is the act of every party to that conspiracy; and therefore the charge and specification that the President was murdered in pursuance of it by the hand of Booth, is a direct and unequivocal charge that he was murdered by every one of the parties to this conspiracy, naming the defendants by name.

Mr. Ewing: I understand... but I renew my inquiry, whether these persons are charged with the crime of conspiracy alone, and that these acts of murdering, assaulting, and lying in wait, were merely acts done in execution of that conspiracy.

Mr. Bingham (interrupting): And not crimes?

Mr. Ewing: Or whether they are charged with four distinct crimes in this one charge?

Mr. Bingham: "Where parties are indicted for a conspiracy, and the execution thereof, it is but one crime at the common law. And that as many... overt acts in the execution of the conspiracy as they are guilty of, may be laid in the same count."

Mr. Ewing: It is then, I understand, one crime with which they are charged.

Mr. Bingham: One crime all round, with various parts performed.

Mr. Ewing: The crime of conspiracy.

Mr. Bingham: It is the crime of murder as well. It is not simply conspiring but executing the conspiracy treasonably and in aid of the Rebellion.

Mr. Ewing: I should like an answer to my question, if it is to be given: How many crimes are my clients charged with and being tried for? I cannot tell.

Mr. Bingham: We have told you, it is all one transaction.

General Ewing, not being able to get an answer intelligible to himself to the first question, then respectfully asked an answer to the second: By what code or statute the crime was defined and the punishment provided?

The Judge-Advocate: I think the common law of war will reach that case. This is a crime which has been committed in the midst of a great civil war, in the capital of the country, in the camp of the Commander-in-Chief of our armies, and if the common law of war cannot be enforced against criminals of that character, then I think such a code is in vain in the world.

 Mr. Ewing: Do you base it, then, only on the law of nations?

 The Judge-Advocate: The common law of war.

 Mr. Ewing: Is that all the answer to the question?

 The Judge-Advocate: It is the one I regard as perfectly appropriate to give.

 Mr. Ewing: I am as much in the dark now as to that as I was in reference to the other inquiry.

It is significant that the ready Special Judge-Advocate rendered no aid to his colleague on the latter branch of the inquiry.

According to the theory of the prosecution, then, Mary E. Surratt was tried, as a co-conspirator of Jefferson Davis and seven of his agents, of the seven men tried with her, and of Booth and her own son, for the crime of "traitorous conspiracy" to murder the President, Vice-President, Secretary of State and Lieutenant-General, of the United States; and for the following crimes committed in pursuance thereof:

1. Assassination of the President, with Booth.

2. Attempt to murder the Secretary of State, his two sons and two attendants (five crimes instead of one), with Payne.

3. Lying in wait to kill the Vice-President, with Atzerodt.

4 Lying in wait to kill the Lieutenant-General, with O'Laughlin.

Four separate species of crimes, beside the generic one of "traitorous conspiracy." And she, a citizen, a non-combatant, a woman, was tried on this five-fold, omnibus charge, jointly with seven men, under "the common law of war"!

On the 16th of June (Friday), Mr. Clampitt read the argument of Reverdy Johnson against the jurisdiction of the Commission – one of the most cogent and convincing ever delivered in a court of justice.

The Supreme Court of the United States, subsequently (December, 1866), in deciding the Milligan case, did but little more than reiterate the propositions maintained by this great lawyer.

He opened his address by reminding the Court that the question of their jurisdiction to try and sentence the accused was for the Court alone to decide, and that no mandate of the President, if in fact and in law the Constitution did not tolerate such tribunals in such cases, could protect any member of the Commission from the consequences of his illegal acts. He then advanced and proved the following propositions: that none but military offenses are subject to the jurisdiction of military courts, and that the offenders when they commit such offenses must be subject to military jurisdiction – in other words, must belong to the army or navy; that the President himself had no right to constitute military courts of his own motion, but that such power must first be exercised by Congress under the constitutional grant to that body to make rules for the government and regulation of the land and naval forces; that, by the fifth and sixth amendments of the Constitution, every person, except those belonging to the land or naval forces or to the militia in active service in time of war, and, being such, committing a military or naval crime, is guaranteed an investigation by a grand jury as a preliminary to trial, and a speedy and public trial by an impartial jury. He then took up and examined the grounds on which the jurisdiction of the Commission was sought to be maintained. Calling the Court's attention to the constitutional provision that, if the institution of such Commission was an incident to the war power, that power was lodged exclusively in Congress and not at all in the President, and, therefore, Congress only could authorize such tribunals, he showed that, neither by the articles of war nor by the two acts, relied on, passed during the Rebellion, had Congress ever authorized any such tribunal; and that a military commission like the present and under present circumstances "is not to be found sanctioned, or the most remotely recognized, or even alluded to, by any writer on military law in England or the United States, or in any legislation of either country."

And, in this connection, he pronounced the suggestion that the civil courts and juries of the District of Columbia could not safely be relied upon for the trial of these cases, "an unjust reflection upon the judges, upon the people, upon the marshal, an appointee of the President, by whom the juries were summoned, and upon our civil institutions themselves;" and he closed his remarks upon this branch of his subject by saying that the foregoing suggestion,

> upon another ground, is equally without force. It rests on the idea that the guilty only are ever brought to trial; that the only object of the Constitution and laws in this regard is to afford the means to establish alleged guilt; that accusation, however made, is to be esteemed *prima facie* evidence of guilt, and that the Executive should be armed, without other restriction than his own discretion, with all the appliances deemed by him necessary to make the presumption from such evidence conclusive. Never was there a more dangerous theory. The peril to the citizen from a prosecution so conducted, as illustrated in all history, is so great that the very elementary principles of constitutional liberty, the spirit and letter of the Constitution itself repudiated it.

After depicting the peril to the rights of the citizen of confiding to the option of the Executive the power of substituting a secret for a public tribunal for the trial of offenses, he established the following propositions: That the creation of a Court is an exclusively legislative function; that constitutional guarantees are designed for times of war as well as times of peace; that the power to suspend the writ of Habeas Corpus carries with it only the temporary suspension of the right to inquire into the cause of the arrest, and does not extend in any way over the other rights of the accused. The distinguished advocate then further maintained that, conceding the articles of war provide for a military court like this, yet the offense charged in the present case being nothing less than treason could not under the provision of the Constitution, regulating the trial of treason, be tried by a military commission; and, also, that under the articles of war persons who were not and never had been in the army were not subject to military law. And, in order to illustrate this branch of his argument as forcibly as possible, passing in review the guaranteed and historic rights of accused persons on trials before civil courts, he arrayed the open and flagrant violations of these rights which had been permitted by the Commission on the present trial: First, in the character of the pleadings, which for indefiniteness and duplicity would not have been tolerated by any civil tribunal. Second, as to the rules of evidence, which, according to the Judge-Advocate, allowed proof of separate and distinct offenses alleged to have been committed, not only by the parties on trial, but by other persons, and which the accused, however innocent, could not be supposed able to meet. Third, he quoted Lord Holt to show that in a civil court "these parties could not have been legally fettered during their trial." Referring to the row of miserable beings weighed down with shackles as they had entered the court-room, as they confronted their epauletted judges, and as they departed to their solitary cells, day by day, for more than a month, he repeated the words of the great jurist, then 200 years old:

> Hearing the clanking of chains, though no complaint was made to him, he said, "I should like to know why the prisoner is brought in ironed. Let them be instantly knocked off. When prisoners are tried they should stand at their ease."

Then, characterizing the claim, that martial law prevailing in the District of Columbia therefore warranted the Commission, as alike indefensible and dangerous, and at the same time irrelevant because martial law had never been proclaimed and the civil courts were in the full and undisturbed exercise of all their functions, the counsel drove this point home as follows:

> We learn, and the fact is doubtless true, that one of the parties, the very chief of the alleged conspiracy, has been indicted, and is about to be tried before one of those courts. If he, the alleged head and front of the conspiracy, is to be and can be so tried, upon what ground of right, of fairness or of policy, can the parties who are charged to have been his mere instruments be deprived of the same mode of trial?

At the close of his speech he recurs to the warning that the President's command can furnish no justification to the members of the tribunal. If their function were only to act as aides to the President to enable him to discharge his prerogative of punishment, and is to that extent legal, then it is only so because the President might have dispensed with the Court altogether, and ordered the punishment of the culprits without any formal trial.

No, he warned them, in the most courtly and courteous manner, they could not shield themselves behind the President.

> Responsibility to personal danger can never alarm soldiers who have faced... death on the battle-field. But there is a responsibility that every gentleman, be he soldier or citizen, will constantly hold before him and make him ponder – responsibility to the constitution and laws of his country and an intelligent public opinion – and prevent his doing anything knowingly that can justly subject him to the censure of either. I have said that your responsibility is great. If the Commission under which you act is void and confers no authority, whatever you may do may involve the most serious personal liability.

He then cited the case of Governor Wall, hung in London in 1802 for murder – a soldier, under his government in the island of Goree, having been whipped to death by sentence of a regimental court-martial, twenty years before.

> In that instance want of jurisdiction in the court-martial was held to be fatal to its judgment as a defense for the death that ensued under it. In this, if the Commission has no jurisdiction, its judgment for the same reason will be of no avail, either to Judges, Secretary of War, or President, if either shall be called to a responsibility for what may be done under it.

The learned counsel then added, "The opinion I have endeavored to maintain is believed to be the almost unanimous opinion of the profession and certainly is of every judge or court who has expressed any."

And he cited the then recent charge of Judge Bond to the grand jury at Baltimore, in which the Judge declared in reference to such military commissions as the present, that, "Such persons exercising such unlawful jurisdiction are liable to indictment by you as well as responsible in civil actions to the parties."

And he quoted to the Court that portion of the charge of Judge Rufus W. Peckham to a grand jury in New York City, delivered during the progress of this very trial, wherein the right of a military commission to try was denied:

> A great crime has lately been committed that has shocked the civilized world. Every right-minded man desires the punishment of the criminals, but he desires that punishment to be administered according to law, and through the judicial tribunals of the country. No star-chamber court, no secret inquisition, in this nineteenth century, can ever be made acceptable to the American mind....
>
> Grave doubts, to say the least, exist in the minds of intelligent men, as to the constitutional right of the Military Commission at Washington to sit in judgment upon the prisoners now on trial for their lives before that tribunal. Thoughtful men feel aggrieved that such a commission should be established in this free country, when the war is over, and when the common law courts are open and accessible to administer justice according to law, without fear or favor....
>
> The unanimity with which the leading press of our land has condemned this mode of trial ought to be gratifying to every patriot.

On the twenty-third, General Ewing, too, assailed the jurisdiction of the Court in a short but powerful speech from which are taken the following extracts:

> The jurisdiction of the Commission has to be sought *dehors* the Constitution, and against its express prohibition. It is, therefore, at least of doubtful validity. If that jurisdiction do not exist; if the doubt be resolved against it by our judicial tribunals, when the law shall again speak, the form of trial by this unauthorized Commission cannot be pleaded in justification of the seizure

of property or the arrest of persons, much less the infliction of the death penalty. In that event, however fully the recorded evidence may sustain your findings, however moderate may seem your sentences, however favorable to the accused your rulings on the evidence, your sentence will be held in law no better than the rulings of Judge Lynch's courts in the administration of lynch law.

Our judicial tribunals, at some future day... will be again in the full exercise of their constitutional powers, and may think, as a large proportion of the legal profession think now, that your jurisdiction in these cases is an unwarranted assumption; and they may treat the judgment which you pronounce and the sentence you cause to be executed, as your own unauthorized acts.

Conviction may be easier and more certain in this Military Commission, than in our constitutional courts. Inexperienced as most of you are in judicial investigation, you can admit evidence which the courts would reject, and reject what they would admit, and you may convict and sentence on evidence which those courts would hold to be wholly insufficient. Means, too, may be resorted to by detectives, acting under promise or hope of reward, and operating on the fears or the cupidity of witnesses, to obtain and introduce evidence, which cannot be detected and exposed in this military trial, but could be readily in the free, but guarded, course of investigation before our regular judicial tribunals. The Judge-Advocate, with whom chiefly rests the fate of these citizens, is learned in the law, but from his position he can not be an impartial judge, unless he be more than a man. He is the prosecutor in the most extended sense of the word. As in duty bound, before this court was called, he received the reports of detectives, pre-examined the witnesses, prepared and officially signed the charges, and, as principal counsel for the Government, controlled on the trial the presentation, admission and rejection of evidence. In our courts of law, a lawyer who has heard his client's story, if transferred from the bar to the bench, may not sit in the trial of the cause, lest the ermine be sullied through the partiality of counsel. This is no mere theoretical objection – for the union of prosecutor and judge works practical injustice to the accused. The Judge-Advocate controls the admission and rejection of evidence – knows what will aid and what will injure the case of the prosecution, and inclines favorably to the one and unfavorably to the other. The defense is met with a bias of feeling and opinion on the part of the judge who controls the proceedings of the Court, and on whom, in great measure, the fate of the accused depends, which morals and law alike reject.

Whatsoever else may be pleaded in excuse or palliation of the acts of the Commission, it can never be said that its members were driven on by an overpowering sense of their duty as soldiers, in blind ignorance of the Constitution and the law. Each and every officer was made fully aware of his awful responsibility and apprised of the precarious footing of his authority.

CHAPTER SEVEN
The Charge of Judge Bingham

From the sixteenth to the twenty-seventh of June the time was consumed by the summing up of the several counsel for the prisoners on the facts disclosed by the evidence; and on the last mentioned day and the succeeding one, Special Judge-Advocate Bingham delivered his address in answer to all the foregoing pleas, both as to the jurisdiction of the Court and also as to the merits of the case.

This long, carefully prepared and yet impassioned speech may be fairly considered as embodying the very proof-charge of the prosecution. Indeed, under the rules of military procedure, it occupies the place and performs the functions of the judge's charge in the common-law courts. As such, it deserves a closer analysis and a more extended examination than can be given to it here. The briefest and most cursory review, however, will suffice to show its tone and temper.

After a solemn asseveration of his desire to be just to the accused, and a warning to the Court that "a wrongful and illegal conviction or a wrongful and illegal acquittal... would impair somewhat the security of every man's life and shake the stability of the Republic," the learned advocate specifically declares, that the charge "is not simply the crime of murdering a human being" but a "combination of atrocities," committed as charged upon the record, "in pursuance of a treasonable conspiracy entered into by the accused with one John Wilkes Booth, and John H. Surratt, upon the instigation of Jefferson Davis, Jacob Thompson, George N. Sanders and others, with intent thereby to aid the existing Rebellion and subvert the constitution and laws of the United States."

A denunciation of the Rebellion as "itself simply a criminal conspiracy and a gigantic assassination"; the following glowing period – "Now that their battalions of treason are broken and flying before the victorious legions of the republic, the chief traitors in this great crime against your government secretly conspire with their hired confederates to achieve by assassination what they in vain attempt by wager of battle" – and the unequivocal announcement that "it is for this secret conspiracy in the interest of the Rebellion, formed at the instigation of the chief in that rebellion, and in pursuance of which the acts charged and specified are alleged to have been done, and with the intent laid, that the accused are upon trial": finish the exordium.

The speaker then tackles the question of jurisdiction, which, he remarks by the way, "as the Court has already overruled the plea," he would pass over in silence, "but for the fact that a grave and elaborate argument has been made by the counsel for the accused, not only to show want of jurisdiction, but to arraign the President of the United States before the country and the world as a usurper of power over the lives and the liberties of the prisoners."

He dexterously evades the force of the argument that the civil courts of the District were open when the crime was committed, by asserting that "they were only open... and are only open at this hour by force of the bayonet;" and he claims that the President acting by a military force had as much right to try the co-conspirators of Booth, as to pursue, capture and kill the chief criminal himself; which, if true, leads us into the maintenance of the monstrous doctrine that the President by a summary order might have strung up the culprits without the interposition of any court. He then enters upon an argument to show that the Commission, from the very nature of its organization, cannot decide that it is no Court, and he ridicules the idea that these nine subordinate military officers could question the authority of their Commander-in-Chief.

In this connection, he gently rebukes Mr. Ewing for his bold statement to the Commission: "You, gentlemen, are no court under the Constitution!" reminding him that "not many months since he was a general in the service of the country and as such in his department in the West proclaimed and enforced martial law;" and asks him whether he is "quite sure he will not have to answer for more of these alleged violations of the rights of citizens than any of the members of the Court?"

He professes his high regard for General Ewing as a military commander who has made a "liberal exercise of this power," and facetiously wishes "to know whether he proposes, by his proclamation of the personal responsibility awaiting all such usurpations," that he himself shall be "drawn and quartered."

After disposing of General Ewing in this gingerly manner, he compensates himself for the slight restraint by pouring the vials of his unstinted wrath upon Reverdy Johnson; representing him as "denouncing the murdered President and his successor," as making "a political harangue, a partisan speech against his government and country, thereby swelling the cry of the armed legions of sedition and rebellion that but yesterday shook the heavens." He characterizes one of the most temperate and dignified of arguments as "a plea in behalf of an expiring and shattered rebellion," and "a fit subject for public condemnation."

He calls upon the people to note,

> That while the learned gentleman [Mr. Johnson], as a volunteer, without pay, thus condemns as a usurpation the means employed so effectually to suppress this gigantic insurrection, the New York *News*, whose proprietor, Benjamin Wood, is shown by the testimony upon your record to have received from the agents of the rebellion $25,000, rushes into the lists to champion the

cause of the rebellion, its aiders and abettors, by following to the letter his colleague [Mr. Johnson], and with greater plainness of speech, and a fervor intensified doubtless by the $25,000 received, and the hope of more, denounces the Court as a usurpation and threatens the members with the consequences.

And he interrupts his tirade against one of the greatest men this country has produced to burst forth into the following grandiloquent apostrophe:

> Youngest born of the Nations! Is she not immortal by all the dread memories of the past – by that sublime and voluntary sacrifice of the present, in which the bravest and noblest of her sons have laid down their lives that she might live, giving their serene brows to the dust of the grave, and lifting their hands for the last time amidst the consuming fires of battle!

After a brief defense of the secret sessions of the Commission, the learned advocate enters upon his circumstantial reply to the argument of Mr. Johnson, into which it is not worth while to follow him, as the main points of his contention have been rendered obsolete by the Supreme Court of the United States.

Suffice it to say, he holds that the President of the United States has the power, of his own motion, to declare martial law in time of war, over the whole United States, whether the States are within the theatre of the war or not; and that President Lincoln exercised this power by his proclamation of September, 1862, by virtue of which martial law prevailed over the whole North, including, of course, the District of Columbia, on the day of the assassination; and, farther, that certain subsequent acts of Congress, though not in express terms yet by fair implication, had ratified the proclamation.

He contends, in consequence, that "nothing can be clearer than that citizen and soldier alike, in time of civil or foreign war, are triable by military tribunals for all offences of which they may be guilty, in the interest of, or in concert with the enemy;" and that "these provisions, therefore, of your Constitution for indictment

The Charge of Judge Bingham 75

and trial by jury in civil courts of *all crimes* are... silent and inoperative in time of war when the public safety requires it."

Listen to this judicial expounder of constitutional law!

> Here is a conspiracy organized and prosecuted by armed traitors and hired assassins, receiving the moral support of thousands in every State and district, who pronounced the war for the Union a failure, and your now murdered but immortal Commander-in-Chief a tyrant.
>
> It is in evidence that Davis, Thompson, and others... agreed and conspired with others to poison the fountains of water which supply your commercial metropolis, and thereby murder its inhabitants; to secretly deposit in the habitation of the people and in the ships in your harbor inflammable materials, and thereby destroy them by fire; to murder by the slow and consuming torture of famine your soldiers, captives in their hands; to import pestilence in infected clothes to be distributed in your capital and camps, and thereby murder the surviving heroes and defenders of the Republic.
>
> I claim that the Constitution itself... by express terms, has declared whatever is necessary to make the prosecution of the war successful, may be done, and ought to be done, and is therefore constitutionally lawful.
>
> Who will dare to say that in the time of civil war no person shall be deprived of life, liberty and property, without due process of law? This is a provision of your Constitution, than which there is none more just and sacred in it; it is, however, only the law of peace, not of war.
>
> In time of war the civil tribunals of justice are wholly or partially silent, as the public safety may require;... the limitations and provisions of the Constitution in favor of life, liberty and property are therefore wholly or partially suspended.

He makes allusion to the recent re-election of President Lincoln, as ratifying any doubtful exercise of power by him:

> The voice of the people, thus solemnly proclaimed, by the omnipotence of the ballot... ought to be accepted, and will be accepted, I trust, by all just men, as the voice of God.

He concludes his plea in favor of the jurisdiction of the Commission, by declaring that for what he had uttered in its favor "he will neither ask pardon nor offer apology," and by quoting Lord Brougham's speech in defence of a bill before the House of Lords empowering the Viceroy of Ireland to apprehend and detain all Irishmen *suspect* of conspiracy.

The Special Judge-Advocate then proceeds to sum up the evidence, in doing which he leaves nothing to the free agency of the Court. He, first, by a review of the testimony of the Montgomeries and Conovers, proves to his own and, presumably, to the Court's satisfaction, that "Davis, Thompson, Cleary, Tucker, Clay, Young, Harper, Booth and John H. Surratt did combine and conspire together in Canada to kill and murder Abraham Lincoln, Andrew Johnson, Wm. H. Seward and Ulysses S. Grant."

> Surely no word further need be spoken to show that John Wilkes Booth was in this conspiracy; that John H. Surratt was in this conspiracy; and that Jefferson Davis, and his several agents named, in Canada, were in this conspiracy.
> Whatever may be the conviction of others, my own conviction is that Jefferson Davis is as clearly proven guilty of this conspiracy as is John Wilkes Booth, by whose hand Jefferson Davis inflicted the mortal wound upon Abraham Lincoln.

After such utterances as these, it is hardly necessary to state that this impartial Judge declares every single person on trial, as well as John H. Surratt, guilty beyond the shadow of a doubt.

> That John H. Surratt, George A. Atzerodt, Mary E. Surratt, David E. Herold, and Louis Payne entered into this conspiracy with Booth, is so very clear upon the testimony, that little time need be occupied in bringing again before the Court the evidence which establishes it.
> It is almost imposing upon the patience of the Court to consume time in demonstrating the fact, which none conversant with the testimony of this case can for a moment doubt, that John

H. Surratt and Mary E. Surratt were as surely in the conspiracy to murder the President as was John Wilkes Booth himself.

He lets out the secret that the mother is on trial as a substitute for her son, whom the Secretary of War and the Bureau of Military Justice had failed to capture, by saying, "Nothing but his conscious coward guilt could possibly induce him to absent himself from his mother, as he does, upon her trial."

After having reiterated over and over again, with all the authority of his office, what he had for hours endeavoured to enforce by all the resources of his intellect, that the guilt "of all these parties, both present and absent" is proved "beyond any doubt whatever," and "is no longer an open question;" he closes by formally, and with a very cheap show of magnanimity, leaving "the decision of this dread issue" to the Court.

CHAPTER EIGHT
The Verdict, Sentence and Petition

  With the loud and repeated denunciations of this elaborate and vindictive harangue, full as it was of rhetorical appeals to the members of the Commission to avenge the murder of "their beloved Commander-in-Chief," and of repeated and most emphatic assurances of the undoubted guilt of each and every one of the prisoners, as well as of all their alleged accomplices, still ringing in the ear of the Court; the room is for the last time cleared of spectators, counsel for the prisoners and reporters; the mournful procession of the accused marches for the last time from the dock to their solitary cells, their fetters clanking as they go; and the Commission meets to deliberate upon its verdict. But who remains in the room, meets with the Court and participates in its secret and solemn deliberations? Who but Colonel Burnett, the officer who had so zealously conducted the preliminary examinations of the witnesses and marshalled the evidence for the prosecution? Who but Recorder Joseph Holt, the head of the Bureau of Military Justice, the left hand of Stanton as Baker was his right? Who but John A. Bingham, the Special Judge-Advocate, who had so mercilessly conducted the trial, assailing counsel, browbeating witnesses for the defense, declaring that all participants in the Rebellion were virtually guilty of the assassination, and who had just closed his long speech, in which he had done his utmost to stir up the Commission to the highest pitch of loyalty, unreasoning passion and insatiable desire for vengeance?

Where can we look in the history of the world for a parallel to such a spectacle? A woman of refinement and education, thrown together in one mass with seven men, to be tried by nine soldiers, for the crime of conspiring with Jefferson Davis, the arch-enemy of every member of the tribunal, to kill, and killing, the beloved Commander-in-Chief of every member of the tribunal; three experienced criminal lawyers eagerly engaging in the task of proving her guilty; pursuing it for days and weeks with the unrelenting vigor of sleuth-hounds; winding up by reiterating in the most solemn manner their overwhelming conviction of her guilt; and then all three being closeted with the Court to take part in making up the doom of death!

And here let us pause to consider one feature of the trial and of the summing up of Judge Bingham, which has not yet been noticed because it deserves special and prominent remark.

It appeared from the testimony on the part of the prosecution, unmistakably, that, during the fall of 1864 and the winter of 1864-5, Booth was brooding over a wild plot for the capture of the President (either on one of his drives, or in the theatre, where the lights were to be turned off), then hurrying off the captive to lower Maryland, thence across the Potomac, and thence to Richmond; thereby to force an exchange of prisoners, if not, possibly, a cessation of the war. It was a plot of the kind to emanate from the disordered brain of a young, spoiled, dissipated and disappointed actor. During this period, Booth made some trifling and miserably inadequate preparations, and endeavored to enlist some of his associates in its execution; and, by his personal ascendency over them, he did in fact entangle, in a more or less vague adhesion to the plot, Arnold, O'Laughlin, Atzerodt, Payne, Herold, John H. Surratt, Lloyd, and, possibly, Dr. Mudd and Weichman.

On the fall of Richmond, and the surrender of Lee, this any-how impracticable scheme was necessarily abandoned. Indeed, the proof showed that Arnold and O'Laughlin had deserted their leader some time before.

It further appeared in the testimony that it was not until after the forced abandonment of this plot and the desertion of most of his adherents, that Booth, plunged as he was into the depths of chagrin and despair because of the collapse of the Rebellion, suddenly, as a mere after-thought, the offspring of a spirit of impotent revenge, seized upon the idea of murder, which was not in fact brought to the birth until the afternoon of the fourteenth, when he was first informed of the promised attendance of President Lincoln and General Grant at the theatre. Now, the existence of the plot to capture, although it looked forth from the evidence steadily into their faces, the Judge-Advocates bound themselves not to recognize. In the first place, such a concession would forever demolish the preconceived theory of the Secretary of War, Colonel Baker and the Bureau of Military Justice, that the conspiracy to murder emanated from the Confederate Government through its Canadian agents, by pointing directly to another plot than the one to kill as that in which these agents had been interested. The horrid monster of a widespread, treasonable conspiracy to overthrow the government, which had been conjured up in the imagination of the Secretary of War and then cherished in the secret recesses of the Bureau of Military Justice, would have immediately shrunk into the comparatively simple case of an assassination of the President and an attempted assassination of the Secretary of State, by two worthless villains suddenly seizing opportunity by the forelock to accomplish their murderous purpose. And, in the next place, the concession of such a plot as a fact would go far to establish the innocence of Mrs. Surratt, Arnold, O'Laughlin and Mudd, as well as that of John H. Surratt, by explaining such suspicious circumstances as the frequent rendezvous of Booth, Payne and others at Mrs. Surratt's house, which practice, as it was proved, ceased altogether on the fall of Richmond and the immediate departure of the son to Canada. To the Judge-Advocates, if not to the Court, any evidence looking towards innocence was most distasteful and unwelcome. They were in no mood to reconcile what they considered the damning proofs of a conspiracy to kill their "beloved Commander-in-Chief" with the innocence of the fettered culprits before them, by admitting a plot to capture, into which nevertheless those same proofs fitted with surprising consistency. Besides, in the eyes of Bingham and Holt, complicity in a plot to capture, although unexecuted, was proof of complicity in the plot to murder, and also of itself deserved death. In this direction, therefore, the Judge-Advocates were mole-eyed. On the contrary, they hailed the slightest indication of guilt with a glow of triumph. In the direction of guilt, they were lynx-eyed.

Consequently, they bent every energy to identify the plot to capture with the plot to kill. They introduced anonymous letters, dropped letters; a letter mailed nearly a month after the assassination directed to J. W. B.; a letter in cipher, purporting to be dated the day after the assassination, addressed to John W. Wise, signed "No Five," found floating in the water at Morehead City, North Carolina, as late as the first of May; this last, the most flagrant violation and cynical disregard of the law of evidence on record.

They did more. They labored to keep out all reference to the plot to capture. And it was for this reason, that the Judge-Advocates deliberately suppressed the diary found on the body of Booth. Its contents demonstrated the existence of the plot to capture.

Instead of allowing the officer who testified to the articles taken from the dead body of Booth to make a detailed statement in response to one general question as to what they were, the examining counsel shows him first the knife, then the pistols, then the belt and holster, then a file with a cork at one end, then a spur, then the carbine, then the bills of exchange, then the pocket-compass; following the exhibition of every article with the interrogatory, "Did you take this from the corpse of the actor?" But no diary was exhibited or even spoken of, although, as has been mentioned, it was carried by this same officer and Colonel Baker to Secretary Stanton on the night following the capture. That these Judge-Advocates had carefully searched through the diary for items they could use against the prisoners, is shown by their calling one of the proprietors of the *National Intelligencer*, as a witness, to contradict the statement that Booth had left a written article, setting forth the reasons for his crime, for publication in that paper – a statement found only in the diary whose very existence they kept secret.

Therefore, when Judge Bingham came to review the evidence, he utterly refused to recognize in the testimony any such thing as a plot to capture; he shut his eyes to it and obstinately ignored it; he scornfully swept it aside as an absurdity it would be waste of time to combat; and he twisted every circumstance which looked to a connection, however remote, with an abandoned plot to kidnap, into a proof, solid and substantial, of complicity in the plot to murder.

And, therefore, when this same thorough-going advocate, with his two emulous associates, proceeded in secret conclave with the members of the Commission to go over the testimony for the purpose of making up their verdict and sentence, he summarily stifled any hint as to the possibility of a plot to capture; he banished from the minds of the Court, if they ever entertained such a purpose, any attempt to reconcile the circumstantial evidence with the existence of such a plot; and, besides, he held it up to the condemnation of those military men as equally heinous and as deserving the same punishment as the actual assassination.

Thus, the presence of these prosecutors during the deliberations of the Court must have exerted a deadly influence (if any influence were necessary) against the prisoners, and benumbed any impartiality and freedom of judgment which might otherwise have lodged in the members of the Commission.

The Commission, with its three attending prosecuting officers, held two secret sessions – Thursday and Friday, the 29th and 30th of June; on the first day from 10 o'clock in the morning until 6 o'clock in the evening, on the second day, probably, during the morning only. The record of the proceedings is meagre, but contains enough to show the lines of the discussion which, in such an unexpected manner through one whole day, prolonged the deliberations of a tribunal organized solely to obey the predetermination of a higher power, and even made necessary an adjournment over night.

There was no difficulty with the verdicts, except in the case of Spangler, over the degree of whose guilt a majority of the Commission presumed for the first time to differ with the Judge-Advocates. They would unite in a conviction of the crime of assisting Booth to escape from the theatre with knowledge of the assassination, but they would go no farther. They would not find him a participant in the "traitorous conspiracy." This poor fellow, as we can see *now*, was clearly innocent of the main charge; but that was no reason, *then*, why the Commission should find him so. There was more testimony pointing to his complicity with Booth on the fatal night than there was against Arnold or O'Laughlin or even Mrs. Surratt; and Judge Bingham, the guardian and guide of the Court, had pronounced it "conclusive and brief." The testimony of the defense, however, appears overwhelmingly convincing, and, moreover, his case was admirably managed by General Ewing.

For all the rest there was no mercy in the verdict. Every one was found guilty of the charge as formulated (eliminating Spangler); that is, in the judgment of the Commission, they had, each and all, been engaged in a treasonable conspiracy with Jefferson Davis, John H. Surratt, John Wilkes Booth and the others named, to kill Abraham Lincoln, President, Andrew Johnson, Vice-President, Wm. H. Seward, Secretary of State, U.S. Grant, Lieutenant-General; and that in pursuance of such conspiracy they (the prisoners) together with John H. Surratt and J. Wilkes Booth, had murdered Abraham Lincoln, assaulted with intent to kill W. H. Seward, and lain in wait with intent to kill Andrew Johnson and U.S. Grant.

This was the deliberate judgment of the Commission as guided by Judge-Advocates Holt, Burnett and Bingham. With the same breath with which they pronounced the guilt of Mrs. Surratt, they pronounced also the guilt of her son, of Jefferson Davis, of Clement C. Clay, of George H. Sanders, of Beverly Tucker. And there can be no doubt that if these men had also been upon trial, they all would have been visited with the same condemnation and would have met the same doom.

The Commission, further, found Herold, Atzerodt, Payne and Arnold guilty of the Specification as formulated (eliminating Spangler); Mrs. Surratt guilty, except that she had not harbored and concealed Arnold or O'Laughlin; Dr. Mudd guilty, except that he had not harbored or concealed Payne, John H. Surratt, O'Laughlin, Atzerodt or Mrs. Surratt; and, strangest of all, they found O'Laughlin guilty of the Specification, *except that he had not lain in wait for General Grant with intent to kill him*, which was the very part in the conspiracy he was charged in the Specification with having undertaken. It should be recollected that, in the first moments of the panic succeeding the assassination, Stanton and his subordinates had included among the objects of the conspiracy, as if to complete its symmetry, the murder of the Secretary of War, himself. Afterwards, probably because of the attitude of Stanton relative to the prosecution, Grant was substituted as the victim of O'Laughlin and not of Booth; Stanton's son having discovered a resemblance of the captured O'Laughlin to the mysterious visitor at his father's house during the serenade on the night of the 13th of April, when General Grant was also present. This pretty romance, the testimony on behalf of O'Laughlin effectually dissipated on the trial, but the indomitable Bingham still insisted on holding the prisoner to a general complicity with the plot. In this instance, as well as in that of Spangler, there may have been some dissension between a majority of the officers and the Judge-Advocates, but, taken altogether, the eight verdicts could not have cost the Commission much time. It was organized to convict, and it did convict.

So that it was not until the Court, having made up its verdicts, proceeded to affix its sentences, that the three advocates, still assisting at the work of death, encountered the unforeseen difficulties which compelled a prolongation of the session. The crime or crimes of which the prisoners were all pronounced guilty (with the possible exception of Spangler's) were capital, and the Secretary of War, on the eve of the assembling of the Commission, had already denounced against such offenses (not excepting Spangler's) the punishment of death.

The sentence, however, under the rules governing military commissions, was wholly within the power of the Court, which, no matter what the nature of the verdict, could affix any punishment it saw fit, from a short imprisonment up to the gallows. Its two-fold function was, like a jury to find a verdict, not only, but, like the judge in a common-law court, to pronounce sentence; and, unlike such a judge, in pronouncing sentence, the Commission was confined within certain limits by no statute. Although the whole proceedings of the Court must be subjected to the final approval of the President, yet its members were clothed alike with the full prerogative of justice and the full prerogative of clemency. There was one limit, however. While a majority could find the verdict and prescribe every other punishment, it required two-thirds of the Commission to inflict the penalty of death. Four officers, therefore, could block the way to the scaffold, and five could mitigate any sentence, to any degree, and for any, or for no reason.

The Commission must have taken up the cases for sentence in the order adopted in the formal Charge. As to the first three – Herold, Atzerodt and Payne – there could have been no dissent or hesitation. The Commission, with hardly a moment's deliberation, must have ratified the judgment of the Judge-Advocates and condemned the prisoners to be hung by the neck until dead. The sentences of death formally declare in every instance that two-thirds of the Commission concur therein, but, as to these three, we can scarcely be in error in stating the Court was unanimous. It was not until the cases of the next three – O'Laughlin, Spangler and Arnold – were reached, that symptoms of dissatisfaction with the sweeping doom of death, so confidently pronounced by Judge Bingham in his charge, first began to show themselves amongst the members of the Court. It seems that now, after having joined with the counsel in pronouncing capital punishment upon the three most prominent culprits, the majority could no longer whet their appetite for blood so as to keep it up to the same fierce edge as that of the Judge-Advocates.

The deviations from the Charge and Specification, the Court had finally prescribed in the verdicts against O'Laughlin and Spangler, were not thought by the prosecutors to be of such importance as to warrant a softening of the sentence. But here the loyalty of some members of the Commission began to falter, and refuse to bear the strain. They had found O'Laughlin guilty of the "traitorous conspiracy," and Spangler guilty of aiding Booth to escape, and Arnold guilty in the same degree as Herold, Atzerodt and Payne, but in none of these cases could the attending advocates extort a two-thirds vote for death. In the case of Spangler, owing, it is said, to the impression made by General Ewing and the influence of General Wallace, they were compelled to allow a sentence of but six years imprisonment. And in the case of the two others – convicted co-conspirators with Booth and Davis though they were – these prosecuting officers had to rest satisfied with but life-long imprisonment.

It was too evident that five members of the Commission had slipped the bloody rein. Three lives had they taken. Henceforth they would stop just this side the grave.

At this point – when the Commission had sentenced to death three men and had just declined to sentence to death two more whom it had pronounced guilty of the same crime – at this point it was, that the sentence of Mary E. Surratt came up for determination.

Now, the crimes of which Arnold had been found guilty were both in law and in fact the same of which she had been found guilty. Even the particular allegation in the Specification is the same in both cases, except some immaterial variance in the verbiage and in the names of co-conspirators.

Of course, it will be presumed that the Commission had found the woman guilty without being pressed. But, equally of course, it will not be doubted that, in determining the sentence which should follow the verdict, the question of exercising the same mercy as the Commission had just exercised in the case of a man convicted of the same crime, must have arisen in the case of the woman. And, the question once having arisen, the first impulse of the majority, if inclined still to mercy, must have been to exert their own unquestioned function, and, as in the other cases, mitigate the sentence themselves. They would have, originally, no motive to thrust upon the President, who was to know comparatively nothing of the evidence, the responsibility of doing that thing, which they themselves who had heard the whole case thought ought to be done, and which in a parallel case they had just done. Even if they believed the woman's crime had a deeper tinge of iniquity than either Arnold's or Mudd's (of which the respective verdicts, however, give no hint), but that nevertheless her age and sex ought to save her from the scaffold, they need not have turned to the President for mercy on such a ground. The woman clothed upon by her age and sex had sat for weeks bodily before them. This very mitigation was what a majority of the Court had power to administer. The reason of the mitigation was a matter of no moment. The Court could commute for "age and sex" as well as the President, and, for that matter, could state the reason for the milder penalty in the sentence itself.

Therefore, it may be taken for granted that here the Judge-Advocates again found that two-thirds of the Court would not concur in the infliction of the death penalty. Nay, that even a majority could not be obtained. Five out of the nine officers announced themselves in favor of imprisonment for life.

Here, indeed, was a coil! The prosecutors were at their wits' ends. And lo! when they passed on to consider the last case, that of Dr. Mudd, the same incomprehensible reluctance to shed more blood did but add to their discomfiture. The verdict indeed had been easily obtainable, but the coveted death-sentence would not follow. The whole day had been spent in these debatings. The expedient of adjourning over to the next day, perhaps, was now tried; and the dismayed Judge-Advocates, with but three out of the eight heads they had made so sure of, and their "female fiend" likely to slip the halter, hurry away to consult with their Chief.

Edwin M. Stanton, as he had presided over the whole preparatory process, so too had kept watch over the daily progress of the trial from afar. Every evening his zealous aide-de-camps made report for the day and took their orders for the morrow.

After the death of Booth and the escape of John H. Surratt, the condemnation to death of the mother of the fugitive had become his one supreme aim.

The condemnation of the other prisoners was to him either a matter of no doubt or was a minor affair. Three heads of the band of assassins stood out in bloody prominence – Booth, John H. Surratt and Payne. The first had been snatched from his clutches by a death too easy. Payne, with hand-cuffs and fetters and chains and ball and hood, he might be confident, could not evade his proper doom. Surratt, by the aid of some inscrutable, malignant power, had contrived to baffle all the efforts of his widespread and mighty machinery of military and detective police. But he had the mother, the friend of Booth and the entertainer of Payne; and she, the relentless Secretary with his accordant lackeys had sworn, should not fail to suffer in default of the self-surrender of her son. She, moreover, was to be made an example and a warning to the women of the South, who, in the judgment of these three patterns of heroism, had "unsexed" themselves by cherishing and cheering fathers, brothers, husbands and sons on the tented field.

In the conclave which Stanton and his two co-adjutors held, either during the recesses of the prolonged session of the first day, or most likely during the night of the adjournment, it was resolved, that if the manly reluctance of five soldiers to doom a woman to the scaffold could be overcome in no other way, to employ as a last resort the *"suggestion,"* that the Court formally condemn her to death, and then, as a compromise, the soft-hearted five petition the President to commute – the three plotters trusting to the chances of the future, with the petition in their custody and the President under their dominion, to render ineffectual this forced concession to what they scorned as a weak sentimentalism. This suggestion of what was in truth a most extraordinary device – a petition to the President to do what the Court could do itself – could not have emanated from the merciful majority of the Court, which subsequently did sign the fatal document. *They*, at least, were sincere, and, if let alone, would have proceeded immediately to embody their own clemency in a formal sentence, as they had done with O'Laughlin and Arnold, and as they were about to do with Mudd. Had there been but one, or two, or three dissentients, so that they were powerless in the face of two-thirds of the Commission; or even had there been four – a number sufficient to block a death-sentence but not sufficient to dictate the action of the Court, then, indeed, recourse to the clemency of the Executive might have been a natural proceeding. But a clear majority had no need to look elsewhere for a power of commutation which they themselves possessed in full vigor, and which, in all probability, after the first three death-penalties, they had determined to apply in every one of the other cases. Neither could the suggestion have been made by one of the minority, because none of them signed the petition to the last. The four must have been steadfast and uncompromising for blood. The whole scheme proceeded from a quarter outside the Court – a quarter which, on the one hand, was possessed by an overmastering revengeful passion, such as was required to point the five officers to a seeming source of mercy to which they might appeal and thus avoid the exercise of their own prerogative in antagonism to their four brethren, and, on the other hand, harbored some secret knowledge or malign intent that the petition would or should be, in fact, an empty form; from a quarter, in short, where the desire for the condemnation to death of Mrs. Surratt was all-controlling and where the condition of the President was well known. They, who suggested the death-sentence and the petition as a substitute for the milder penalty, were surely all on the side of death, and hoped, if they did not believe, that the prayer of the petition would be of no avail; else they would not have adopted such a circuitous method to do what the five officers could immediately have accomplished themselves. In one word, the contrivers of the device of petition were not those who desired to save the bare life of the convicted she-conspirator, but were those who would be satisfied with nothing less than her death on the scaffold. The suggestion was wholly sinister and malevolent. On the other hand, the majority of the Court did really desire that her punishment should not exceed that of Arnold, O'Laughlin and Mudd, and they certainly would never have had recourse to a petition to the President, had they not been cheated into believing that that method of proceeding was likely to effectuate what they had full power to do. Never would these five soldiers, or any two of them, have given their voices for the death of this woman, had they dreamed for a moment that their signing of the petition was, and was meant to be, but a farce. They would not have played such a ghastly trick under the shadow of the gibbet.

Accordingly, when the Commission reassembled, either after recess or adjournment, the reinvigorated counsellors immediately unfolded their plan. We can almost hear their voices, in that upper room of the Old Penitentiary, as they alternately urge on the Court. Holt, making a merit of yielding in the cases of Spangler, of O'Laughlin, of Arnold and of Mudd, denounces the universal disloyalty of the women of the South, and pleads the necessity of an example.

Bingham, holding up both mother and son as equally deep-dyed in blood with Booth and Payne, both insinuates and threatens at the same time, that, if *"tenderness,"* forsooth, is to be shown because of the age and sex of such a she-assassin, then, for the sake of the blood of their murdered Commander-in-Chief, do not his own soldiers show it, but let his successor take the fearful responsibility.

One of the five gives way, and now there is a majority for death. One more appeal! The life of the woman trembles in the balance. Once more to the breach! The supreme reserve is at last brought forward – an argument much in use with Judge-Advocates in cases of refractory courts-martial, as a last resort – that the President will not allow a hair of her head to be harmed, but that *terror*, terror, is necessary; in this instance, to force the son to quit his hiding place, the life of the mother must be the bait held out to catch the unsurrendering son. We will hang him and then free the woman's neck.

Another vote comes over. Two-thirds at last concur, and her doom is sealed. They sentence "Mary E. Surratt to be hanged by the neck until she be dead." Judge Bingham sits down and embodies the memorable "suggestion" in writing as follows:

[It is without address.]

The undersigned, members of the Military Commission detailed to try Mary E. Surratt and others for the conspiracy and the murder of Abraham Lincoln, late President of the United States, &c., respectfully pray the President, in consideration of the sex and age of the said Mary E. Surratt, if he can, upon all the facts in the case, find it consistent with his sense of duty to the country, to commute the sentence of death, which the Court have been constrained to pronounce, to imprisonment in the penitentiary for life.

Respectfully submitted.

General Ekin copies it on a half-sheet of legal-cap paper, and the five officers, viz.: Generals Hunter, Kautz, Foster and Ekin, and Colonel Tompkins, sign the copy; General Ekin keeping the draft of Bingham as a memento of so gentle an executioner.

The Commission then proceeds to the next and last case, and, again exercising its prerogative of clemency, sentences Dr. Mudd to imprisonment for life. It is now Friday noon. The result of the two-days' secret session, consisting of a succinct statement of the verdict and sentence in every case, in the foregoing order, is redacted into a record. The presiding officer signs, and the Recorder countersigns it. It is placed in the hands of the Judge-Advocate, together with the petition to the President. There is an adjournment without day. The members disperse, and the work of the Military Commission is over.

CHAPTER NINE
The Death Warrant and Execution

      From Friday afternoon, the thirtieth of June, through Saturday, Sunday, Monday and Tuesday, the first four days of July, the record of the findings and sentences remained under the seal of sworn secrecy in the custody of the Judge-Advocate-General. To consummate the work of the Commission, the signature of the President to a warrant approving its action and directing the execution of its judgment was necessary. But, during this interval, as it was given out from the White House, President Johnson was too ill to attend to public business. In the meantime, the city, and even the whole country to its very borders, were agitated by the question: What is to be the fate of Mrs. Surratt? The doom of the male culprits was for the moment forgotten in the intense anxiety over hers.

      Despite the seven-fold seal of secrecy which covered the proceedings of the secret sessions, whispers of a recommendation of mercy filled the air. In the War Department, the main source of anxiety, at the same time, must have been this superfluous paper – the distressing outcome of an unsuspected sentimental weakness in five of our chosen men. After the final adjournment of the Commission, the unobtrusive, unaddressed half-sheet had been fastened to the record of the sentences by the same narrow yellow silk ribbon which held its own sheets together, and to which it now dangled as a last leaf, or back. A safety-valve to the misplaced chivalry of the Court – it had served its purpose, and was henceforth useless. That it should now turn itself into an implement of evil, minister to the cause of rebellion and assassination, cause "Our Own Andy" to flinch at last and thus the she-fiend of the Bureau escape her doom! It would be treason to suffer it. Upon that resolve, the Triumvirate of Stanton, Holt and Bingham had once for all determined. Indestructible, inconcealable, omnipotent, indeed, must that paper be, which could thwart their united purpose.

At length, on the morning of Wednesday, the fifth, Preston King, who, in those days, was a favored guest at the White House, announced in the Judge-Advocate's office that the President was so much better as to be able to sit up; and at a later hour in the day, General Holt, in pursuance of an appointment, started on his solemn errand. The volumes of testimony taken before the Commission by official stenographers, daily reports of which had been furnished, he, of course, did not carry with him. In the interview that was to come, there would be no time and no inclination to read over bulky rolls of examinations and cross-examinations of witnesses. From aught that appears, the President was not expected to read over the evidence, nor was it customary in such cases. It may have been the duty of the Secretary of War or the Attorney-General to scrutinize the testimony, either from day to day or at the close of the trial. But all that the President was supposed to know about the merits of the case appears to have been derived from what any of his Cabinet saw fit to inform him, from what he himself casually and unofficially read, but, especially and principally, from what the Judge-Advocate was now coming to tell him. As to the guilt of the accused, and especially of Mrs. Surratt, his mind had long ago been made up for him by his imperious War Minister, from whose despotic sway he had not as yet recovered energy enough to free himself. He was still in that brief introductory period of his Presidency which may be called his Stanton Apprenticeship; still eager "to make treason odious;" full of threatenings to hang Davis and other Southern leaders. He had not yet awakened from the state of semi-stupefaction into which his sudden and awful elevation seems to have thrown him; and, in this state, he must have been extremely averse to dwelling on any of the circumstances of the assassination to which he owed his high place. The idea of clemency to any one of the band of assassins, male or female, which his War-Secretary's court might convict, would have been intolerable to his imagination and sickening to his sense of security. What Andrew Johnson, at this moment, wanted was to push away from his mind all thoughts of the tragic end of his predecessor, and to allow retributive vengeance to take the most summary course with the least possible knowledge and trouble to himself. And this mood of the presidential mind was well known to the Judge-Advocate-General, as he entered the President's room. He brought with him so much of the record of the proceedings of the Commission as was necessary to the accomplishment of his errand – viz.: the record of the findings and sentences, which the President was to endorse. This document consisted of a few sheets of legal-cap paper fastened together at the top, written on both sides in the fashion of legal papers, i.e., beginning at the top of the first page and, on reaching the bottom, turning up the paper and writing on the back from the bottom to top. It was a document complete in itself, the written record ending on the first page of the last half-sheet – thus leaving blank the remainder of that page and the whole of the obverse side; ample room for the death-warrant. To this record, but forming no part of it, the Petition, as we have said, had been affixed, but in such a manner as to be easily separable without mutilation. He must also have brought with him his official report of the trial – styled "The formal brief review of the case," which was subsequently appended to the regular Report of the Judge-Advocate-General to the Secretary of War and transmitted to the Congress in December following – because it is addressed "To the President," is dated "*July 5, 1865,*" and is signed "J. Holt." It recites the verdicts and sentences; justifies its brevity by referring to "the full and exhaustive" argument of Judge Bingham; certifies to the regularity and fairness of the proceedings; and recommends the execution of the sentences; *but it makes no mention of the Petition, or any "suggestion" of mercy.*

The Judge-Advocate could have anticipated no difficulty in obtaining the approval of the President, conscious as he was that the grounds of such approval were to be furnished to the President by himself. The approval being had, the fixing of the day of execution could cause no disagreement. His only possible source of embarrassment was the petition for commutation. But it would be strange, indeed, if a few apt words could not further emasculate the mild, hypothetical language in which his colleague, Bingham, had seen fit to clothe that paper.

He found the President "alone," and (as he himself says) "waiting for" him, "very pale, as if just recovered from a severe illness."

"Without delay" he "proceeded to discharge the duty which brought" him "into his presence." What took place at this "confidential interview" (as Holt calls it) can never be precisely known; the distinguished interlocutors having subsequently risen into unappeasable quarrel over the presence or absence of the petition, and given contradictory versions. Whatever the truth may be, it is evident that everything went smoothly at the moment. The Judge-Advocate was not disappointed. No difficulty was encountered. What was done was done quickly and at once. The record may have been read over; but this was hardly necessary, as the bare mention of the several sentences would convey a correct summary of its contents. He may have read the "brief review of the case" he had prepared. As Judge Holt relates, he said to the President, "frankly, as it was his official duty to do," that in his judgment "the proceedings of the Court were regular, and its findings and sentences justified by the evidence, and that the sentences should be enforced." And this was what he had written in his "Brief Review." What more could the successor of the murdered Lincoln want? His approval must have been spontaneous and immediate. As Holt says, "at that time Mr. Johnson needed no urging." Mention may have been made of the curious weakness infecting some members of "our Court" towards the wicked woman, who, as Johnson seems then to have thought, "had kept the nest that hatched the egg;" but only to be scouted by both Judge-Advocate and President as most reprehensible and actually *disloyal*.

Their unanimity over the salutary effect of the hanging of this one woman on the female rebels was more than fraternal. And it is probable that no more explicit mention of an actual petition was made by Judge Holt in his conversation with the President than was made in his written report to the President, dated the same day, and which he had with him at the time.

The day of execution was fixed upon with the same alacrity. "Make it as soon as possible, so that the disagreeable business may be over; say the day after to-morrow – Friday, the seventh." And, thereupon, everything being agreed upon, Judge Holt turns over the papers to the last page of the record and spreads it upon the table. Beginning, a few lines below the signature of "D. Hunter, President" which closes the record, with the date, "Executive Mansion, July 5th, 1865," "with his own hand" he writes out the death warrant. As this includes the approval of the sentences, the appointment of the day and hour of execution, and the designation of the place of confinement of those condemned to imprisonment, the bottom of the page is reached before he completes his task. If he had turned up the page and continued his writing on the obverse side from the bottom down, as all the foregoing had been written, then the petition of mercy, unaddressed as it was, would have been, if still attached, directly beneath the eye of the President as he signed the death-warrant. But, as now appears from the record itself, the careful Judge-Advocate did not turn up the page from the bottom. On the contrary, reverting to the layman's way of writing papers, he whisks the whole record over, and continues the writing of the death-warrant on the back of the last half-sheet of the record *from the top to the bottom* – by this change of method, either throwing the petition under the leaves of the record, or, if disengaged, leaving it *upside down*.

When he has thus finished his draft he shoves it over to the President. The President signs it with tremulous hand. The "confidential interview" is at an end; and the Judge-Advocate, taking up the papers, hurries out and over to the Department of War.

At this moment the petition disappears from view. We hear no more of it. Thrust as a convenient succedaneum into the hands of the majority of the Commission, ignored, suppressed or slurred over when before the President, it had served its pitiful purpose. Neither the Adjutant-General nor any of his clerks, appear to have noticed it, although the record must have been copied more than once in his office. It seems to have sunk suddenly into oblivion; its very existence became the subject of dispute. It was omitted from the authorized published proceedings of the Commission. It was omitted from the annual report of the Judge-Advocate. The disloyal paper must have been laid alongside the suppressed "Diary," there to repose unseen until the Impeachment of Johnson and the Trial of Surratt summoned them together into the light of day.

On the morning of Thursday, the sixth day of July, the six days ominous silence of the War-Department is broken. An order issues from the Adjutant-General's office which, bearing date the day before and reciting the findings and death-sentences of the Commission and the death-warrant of the President, commands Major-General Hancock to see execution done, on the seventh, between the hours of ten and two.

This order was read to Mrs. Surratt at noon. She had all along been encouraged to hope. She, herself, had never been able to realize the possibility of a capital condemnation in her own case. And, here, suddenly, was Death, with violence and shame, within twenty-four hours. She sank down under the blow. In faltering accents she protested that she had no hand in the murder of the President, and pleaded for a few days more time to prepare for death. During the remainder of the day and throughout the night, she was so prostrated by physical weakness and mental derangement as to necessitate medical aid to keep her alive and sane. The cries of her daughter could be heard in the still darkness outside the prison. At five o'clock in the morning, the mother (with the three condemned men), was removed to a solitary cell on the first floor, preparatory to the execution.

In the meantime, when it first became known that, by the

sentence of the Commission and the direction of the President, Mrs. Surratt was to die by the rope on the same scaffold with Payne, Herold and Atzerodt within twenty-four hours, a chill of despairing terror froze the blood of her relatives and friends, a thrill of consternation swept over the body of the citizens, and dark misgivings disturbed even the most loyal breasts. A stream of supplicants at once set in towards the Executive Mansion – not only friends and acquaintances of the condemned woman, but strangers, high-placed men, and women too, who were haunted by doubts of her guilt and could in some degree realize her agony.

But even this expiring effort of sympathy, the powers behind the President had anticipated. Apprehensive that Andrew Johnson, at the last moment, might yield to distressing importunities for more time, they had already taken measures that their sick man's wish to hear nothing till all was over should be scrupulously respected. Preston King and General James Lane undertook to keep the door and bar all access to the President during the dreadful interval between the promulgation of the sentence and its execution. It was rumored that they, with a congenial crew, held high revelry around their passive Chief in his private apartments. Be this as it may, no supplicant – friend, acquaintance or stranger – was allowed to gain access to the President.

The priests, who had attested upon her trial the good character, the piety and the general worth of their parishioner, instinctively turned their steps to the White House to beg for clemency, or, at least, a respite. They were repulsed from its door. In ghastly mockery, they were told to go to — Judge Holt.

At last, the daughter of the victim made her way to the very threshold of the President's room. Frenzied with grief she assailed the portal with her cries for admission to plead for her dying mother. She was denied admittance. In the extremity of her despair she lay down upon the steps, and, in the name of God, appealed to the President and to the wardens, only to listen to her prayer. The grim guardians of the door held it shut in her face.

Denied, thus, even an appeal to Executive clemency, the friends of the poor woman, as a last most desperate resort, invoked the Constitution of their and her country through the historic writ of Habeas Corpus. On the morning of the day of the execution, they found a judge (Judge Wylie; all honor to his memory!) who had the independence and courage to grant the writ. At half-past eleven, General Hancock appeared before the Judge and made return that by order of the President the Habeas Corpus was suspended and therefore he did not produce the body. The order of the President dated ten o'clock, same morning, was annexed to the return and directed the General to proceed with the execution.

No sooner had the guarantees of the Constitution been, thus, finally set at naught, than the cell-doors were thrown open and the prisoners summoned to their doom. As the enfeebled widow raised her trembling limbs from off the coarse mattress which alone separated her body from the stone floor of her dungeon, she strove, in broken words, to assure the soldiers, who had come to bind her arms behind her back and tie cords around her skirts above and below the knee, of her utter, yet helpless innocence. Her confessor, who stood by her until the last, gently pointed out to her the uselessness of such appeals, at such a moment, and directed her hopes towards Heaven.

Amid the tolling of the bells, sending a shudder through the silent population of the city, and heralded by the tramp of armed men, the death-march of the doomed woman and the doomed men begins. The still breathing men and still breathing woman are clothed already in their shrouds. As she totters first along the corridor, accompanied by her priest and requiring two soldiers to hold her erect, the very extremity of her helplessness and woe bears witness in her favor. Even the bloody Payne, who walks next behind her, has broken through that stolid indifference to his own fate, so remarkable as to indicate insanity, to clear her from all complicity with the assassination. Herold and Atzerodt, who follow, though themselves speechless with terror, seem to wave her mute acquittal, as they stumble along into the swift-coming Darkness. They reach the prison-yard. They mount the high scaffold. They are seated in four chairs facing the four dangling nooses, while the death-warrant is once more read. Their graves, already dug, are in full sight close by. Their coffins stand by the side of the open graves. They are raised up and pushed forward upon the two drops, Herold and Atzerodt on one, Mrs. Surratt and Payne on the other; the half-conscious woman still supported by the two guards. The ropes are adjusted. The hoods drawn over the face. The signal is given. The two drops fall. Surrounded by the unpitying soldiery, headed by the unpitying Hartranft, the woman and the men hang writhing in the agonies of an ignominious death. When pronounced dead, the bodies are cut down. They are laid out on the top of the coffins. A hurried post-mortem examination is made. And, then, at four o'clock in the afternoon, they are inclosed in the coffins and buried side by side. The soldiers depart with flourish of trumpet and beat of drum. Silence descends on the grounds of the old Arsenal; broken only by the pace of the sentinel set to guard the four corpses.

The daughter may beg the stern Secretary to yield up the body of her murdered mother, that she may place it in consecrated ground. But she will beg in vain.

And so ended the fell tragedy. And so did brave soldiers avenge the murder of their "beloved Commander-in-Chief." Methinks their beloved Commander-in-Chief, could his freed spirit have found a mortal voice, would have spurned, with indignant horror, the savage sacrifice of a defenseless woman to appease his gentle shade.

CHAPTER TEN
Was It Not Murder?

And now what shall be said as to this taking of human life?
Maintaining the most rigorous allegiance to the simple unadulterated truth, what can be said? Arraigned at the bar of the common law as expounded by the precedents of centuries, and confronted by plain provisions of the Constitution of the United States, which need no exposition and yet have been luminously expounded; but one thing can be said.

Had Mary E. Surratt the right guaranteed by the Constitution to a trial singly and alone, in a regularly constituted civil court, and by a jury of the vicinage, the individuals of which she might select by challenge, both for cause, in all cases, and without cause to a certain number, before she could be legally convicted of any crime whatever, or be lawfully punished by the most trivial loss of property or the minutest injury to limb, to say nothing of the brutal crushing out of her life? That's the unevadable question which the ages put and will continue to put. And upon its precisely truthful answer, depend the character and color of the acts of every person who had lot or part in the execution of this woman.

On the 21st day of October, 1864 – while the war was still raging – Lambdin P. Milligan, a citizen of the United States and a resident of Indiana, was arraigned before a Military Commission convened by the commanding General of that Military District, at Indianapolis, on the following charges preferred against him by Henry L. Burnett, Judge-Advocate of the Department of the West:

    1. Conspiracy against the Government of the United States.
    2. Affording aid and comfort to the rebels.
    3. Inciting insurrection.
    4. Disloyal practices.
    5. Violation of the laws of war.

There were also specifications, the substance of which was that Milligan had joined and aided a secret society, known as the Order of American Knights or Sons of Liberty, for the purpose of overthrowing the Government and authorities of the United States; had communicated with the enemy; conspired to seize munitions of war in the arsenals, and to liberate prisoners; resisted and encouraged resistance to the draft: at or near Indianapolis, in Indiana, "a State within the military lines of the Army of the United States, and the theatre of military operations, and which had been and was constantly threatened to be invaded by the enemy."

On these charges and specifications, Milligan was subjected to a lengthy trial by this Military Commission which finally found him guilty on all the charges and sentenced him to be hanged. The record was approved by the Commanding General, and then transmitted to President Lincoln, who held it long under advisement, and was so holding it when he was killed. His successor, at about the same time that he summoned the Commission to try Mrs. Surratt, at length approved the findings and ordered the sentence to be executed on Friday, the 19th day of May, 1865.

But this object-lesson to the Commission sitting at that date in the old Penitentiary was intercepted. On the 10th of May, Milligan brought the record before the United States Circuit Court by a petition for his discharge, and, the two judges differing upon the main question of the jurisdiction of the Commission, the cause was certified under the statute to the Supreme Court of the United States; in deference to which action the President suspended the execution. The argument before that high tribunal coming on in the winter of 1865-66, a great array of counsel appeared upon both sides; David D. Field, James A. Garfield and Jeremiah S. Black for the prisoner, and Attorney-General Speed and Benjamin F. Butler for the United States. The counsel for the Government followed the same line as did Judge Bingham in his argument on the "Conspiracy Trial;" the counsel for the prisoner on their side, only enlarging, emphasizing and enforcing the argument of Reverdy Johnson. At the close of the term the Court unanimously decided that the Military Commission had no jurisdiction to try Milligan; that its verdict and sentence were void; and ordered the defendant discharged.

At the next term, the Court handed down two opinions – one the opinion of the Court, read by Judge Davis, in which four of his colleagues concurred, and one by Chief-Justice Chase, in which three of his colleagues concurred. The two opinions agreed that, as matter of law, the President could not of his own motion authorize such a Commission, and that, as matter of fact, the Congress had not authorized such a Commission; and therefore they were at one in their conclusion. But they differed in this; that, whereas the majority of the Court held that not even the Congress could authorize such a Court, the minority, while agreeing that the Congress had not exercised such a power, were of opinion that such a power was lodged in that branch of the Government.

The attempt has often been made to distinguish the case of Mrs. Surratt from that of Milligan by alleging that Washington at the time of the assassination was within the theatre of military operations, and actually under martial law, whereas Indiana at the time of the Commission of Milligan's alleged offenses was not.

Now, it must be admitted that at the time of the murder of President Lincoln the war had swept far away from the vicinity of the Capital. There had been no Confederate troops near it since Early's raid in the summer of 1864, and no enemy even in the Shenandoah Valley since October. It must also be admitted, and was, in fact, proved on the trial, that the civil courts were open and in full and unobstructed discharge of their functions. As for the reiterated affirmation of Judge Bingham that the courts were only kept open by the protection of the bayonet; that is precisely what was affirmed by General Butler, in his argument before the Supreme Court, to have been the fact in Indiana.

None of the counsel in the Milligan case claimed that a Military Commission could possibly have jurisdiction to try a simple citizen in a State where there was no war or rumors of war.

> We do fully agree, that if at the time of these occurrences there were no military operations in Indiana, if there was no army there, if there was no necessity of armed forces there... then this Commission had no jurisdiction to deal with the relator, and the question proposed may as well at once be answered in the negative.

They contended, as the very basis of their case, that the acts of Milligan "took place in the theatre of military operations, within the lines of the army, in a State which had been, and then was constantly threatened with invasion."

And, in fact, the record in so many words so stated, and the statement was uncontroverted by the relator.

General Butler with great earnestness put the question:

> If the Court takes judicial notice that the courts are open, must it not also take judicial notice how, and by whose protection, and by whose permission they were so open? that they were open because the strong arm of the military upheld them; because by that power these Sons of Liberty and Knights of the American Circle, who would have driven them away, were arrested, tried and punished.
>
> If the soldiery of the United States, by their arms, had not held the State from intestine domestic foes within, and the attacks of traitors without; had not kept the ten thousand rebel prisoners of war confined in the neighborhood from being released by these Knights and men of the Order of the Sons of Liberty; there would have been no courts in Indiana, no place in which the Circuit Judge of the United States could sit in peace to administer the laws.

Moreover, the opinion of the minority Judges bases their contention that Congress had the power, if it had chosen to exercise it, to authorize such a Military Commission, upon this very fact.

> In Indiana, for example, at the time of the arrest of Milligan and his co conspirators, it is established by the papers in the record, that the State was a military district; was the theatre of military operations, had been actually invaded, and was constantly threatened with invasion. It appears, also, that a powerful secret association, composed of citizens and others, existed within the State, under military organization, conspiring against the draft, and plotting insurrection, the liberation of the prisoners of war at various depots, the seizure of the State and national arsenals, armed co-operation with the enemy, and war against the national government.

Not one of which circumstances (except that it was a military district) can be truthfully predicated of the District of Columbia at the time of the assassination.

As for actual martial law, there was no declaration of martial law claimed for the City of Washington, other than the proclamation of the President which applied as well to Indiana, and, indeed, to the whole North.

We are justified, therefore, in saying, that the Supreme Court of the United States, in this case of Milligan, pronounced the final condemnation of the whole proceedings of the Military Commission which tried and condemned Mary E. Surratt; declaring, with all the solemn force of a determination of the highest judicial tribunal known to this nation, that every one of its acts, from its creation by the President to its transmission of its record of doom to the President, was in direct contravention of the Constitution of the United States and absolutely null and void.

That illustrious Court, speaking by Judge David Davis, thus enunciates the law:

> The Constitution of the United States is a law for rulers

and people, equally in war and in peace, and covers with the shield of its protection all classes of men, at all times, and under all circumstances. No doctrine, involving more pernicious consequences, was ever invented by the wit of man than that any of its provisions can be suspended during any of the great exigencies of government. Such a doctrine leads directly to anarchy or despotism.

From what source did the Military Commission... derive their authority?

It is not pretended that the commission was a court ordained or established by Congress.

They cannot justify on the mandate of the President; because he is controlled by law and has his appropriate sphere of duty, which is to execute not to make the law; and there is no unwritten criminal code to which resort may be had as a source of jurisdiction.

The laws and usages of war can never be applied to citizens in states which have upheld the authority of the government and where the courts are open and their processes unobstructed. And no usage of war could sanction a military trial there for any offence whatever of a citizen in civil life, in nowise connected with the military service. Congress could grant no such power; and to the honor of our national legislature be it said it has never been provoked by the state of the country even to attempt its exercise.

All other persons [i.e., all other than those in the military and naval service citizens of states where the courts are open, if charged with crime, are guaranteed the inestimable privilege of trial by jury. This privilege is a vital principle, underlying the whole administration of criminal justice; it is not held by sufferance, and cannot be frittered away on any plea of state or political necessity.

It is claimed that martial law covers with its broad mantle the proceedings of this Military Commission.

Martial law cannot arise from a threatened invasion. The necessity must be actual and present; the invasion real, such as effectually closes the courts and deposes the civil administration.

Martial law can never exist where the courts are open, and in the proper and unmolested exercise of their jurisdiction. It is also confined to the locality of actual war.

Had the swift process by which this unfortunate woman was hurried to the scaffold been interrupted by a stay to allow a review by the same high tribunal which rescued Milligan from the jaws of death, it cannot be doubted that in her case, as in his, the same conclusions would have been reached, viz.:

1st. "One of the plainest constitutional provisions was, therefore, infringed when" (Mary E. Surratt) "was tried by a court not ordained and established by Congress, and not composed of judges appointed during good behavior."

2nd. "Another guarantee of freedom was broken when" (Mary E. Surratt) "was denied a trial by jury;" that, in her case, as in his, the Court would have set the prisoner free; there would have been no hanging, no felon's grave, and not even an ulterior attempt at a constitutional trial.

For it is remarkable that although the Military tribunal which tried Milligan pronounced him guilty of crimes deserving a traitor's death; the seeming strength of the evidence must have melted away, strangely enough, when subjected to the prospective investigation of constitutional courts, as there was not even a subsequent effort on the part of the Government to call him to account.

Let us add, as a final corollary to this exposition of the Constitution by the Supreme Court, the following remark: that the ground and argument employed by Attorney General Speed in his opinion upon the right of the President to order the trial of the alleged assassins by Military Commission, and by Judge-Advocate Bingham in his address to that Commission, involve a *reductio ad absurdum*, or, rather, a *reductio ad monstrosum*, that is, a *Reductio ad absurdum quia monstrosum*.

For, that ground and that argument, invoked to uphold and sanction the trial of civilians by military commissions, necessarily and inevitably go farther, and proclaim the right of President Johnson, alone, of his own motion and without the interposition of a formal court, whether military commission or drum-head court-martial, to have commanded the immediate execution of every person whom he might believe to be guilty of participation in the assassination of his predecessor or in the presumed attempt upon himself.

The conclusion forced upon us, therefore – the one only thing to be said – is, that the hanging of Mary E. Surratt was nothing less than the crime of murder.

Murder, not only in the case of the private soldiers who dragged her to the scaffold and put the rope about her neck; they, at least can plead the almost irresistible force of military discipline.

But murder, also, in the case of the Major-General whose sword gave the signal for the drop to fall. General and soldiers are in the precise position, before the law, of a mob of Lynchers carrying out the judgment of a Lynch court.

Murder, not only in the case of the one military officer who superintended the details of the execution. He, too, though with much less force, can plead that he was the mere bailiff of what he believed to be a competent Court.

But murder, also, on the part of the nine military officers and the three advocates who tried and sentenced this woman to death. These men, in the forum of the law, stand in the precise position of any nine policemen steered by any three police attorneys in the city of New York, who should dare to try, convict and sentence to death a citizen of that city.

Murder, not only on the part of the Commission and its lawyers; they too might, possibly, plead – though with still diminishing force – that, although they were warned and took the awful responsibility, still they believed in their competency.

But murder, also, in the President of the United States, who appointed the court, approved its findings, and commanded the execution of its sentence. He stands before the law in the same position as though, sweeping aside all empty forms, he had seized a sword and with his own hand cut off the head of the woman, without the mockery of a trial. In our frame of government, there is surely no room for such a twi-formed barbarian-despot, as a President having the power to pick out from the army, of which he is the commander-in-chief, the members of a court to try and punish with death, at his option, any one of the citizens, for an abortive attempt on his own life.

And it was murder, not only in the case of the President; he, too, but with scarcely audible voice, might plead the coercion of his situation – sitting as he did in the seat of the murdered Lincoln.

But it was murder, also, in the Secretary of War, who initiated the iniquitous process, pushed on the relentless prosecution, shut his own ears and the ears of the President to all pleas for mercy, presided like a Moloch over the scaffold, and kept the key of the charnel-house, where, beside the unpitied carcasses of the reputed ruffians forced upon her in her ordeal of torture and in the hour of death, the slaughtered lady lay mouldering in her shroud. Here, at least, the plea of mitigation exhales in a cry like that of Payne, "I was mad!"

Weigh the extenuating circumstances in whatever scale you may; extend as much mercy as possible to those who showed no mercy in their day of power – still, the offense of every one and all, who had hand, part or lot in this work of death, contains every element which, under the most rigorous definition of the law, makes up the Crime of Murder. The killing was there. The unlawful killing was there. The premeditated design to effect death was there. The belief of the perpetrators, that they had a right to kill, or that they were commanded to kill by an overruling power, before a court of law avails not a whit. Ignorance of the constitution as well as the law excuses no man, be he civilian or soldier, President or assassin, War-Minister or Payne.

Murder it essentially was, and as such it should be denounced to the present and future generations.

Garrett Davis told no more than the exact truth when he declared in his place in the Senate of the United States:

> There is no power in the United States, in time of war or peace, that can legitimately and constitutionally try a civilian who is not in the naval or military service of the United States, or in

the militia of a State in the actual service of the United States, by a court-martial or by a military commission. It is a usurpation, and a flagitious usurpation of power for any military court to try a civilian, and if any military court tries a civilian and sentences him to death and he is executed under the sentence, the whole court are nothing but murderers, and they may be indicted in the State courts where such military murders are perpetrated; and if the laws were enforced firmly and impartially every member of such a court would be convicted, sentenced and punished as a murderer.

Although the actual guilt of any of the victims constitutes no legal defense to this fearful charge, yet as the unquestioning obedience which the soldier yields, as a matter of course, to the commands of his superior officer must alleviate, if it do not wipe away, the guilt of the members of the Commission, in the forum of morals; so the ascertainment that the sufferers on the scaffold and in prison, in fact, deserved their doom, cannot but blunt the edge of our condemnation of the iniquity of the trial, as well as weaken our pity for the condemned and our sense of shame over the tyrannous acts of the government.

A word or two, therefore, will be appropriate in respect to the sufficiency of the testimony to establish the guilt of the accused.

I. As to Arnold and O'Laughlin, it may be said in one emphatic word, that there was no evidence at all against them of complicity in the plot to kill. The letter of Arnold to Booth shows, when fairly construed, that, if the writer had conspired with the actor, he conspired to abduct; and, also, for the time being, even that conspiracy he had abandoned. He was at Fort Monroe for the two weeks prior to the assassination. His confession, used on the trial against himself not only but also against O'Laughlin because he was mentioned in it as present at a meeting of the conspirators, was a confession only of a conspiracy to abduct which had been given up. The condemnation of these two men was brought about by the conduct of Judge Bingham, to which we have drawn attention, in systematically shutting his eyes to the existence of any conspiracy to capture, and employing the letter and confession as proof that both these men were guilty of conspiracy to murder.

II. As to Dr. Mudd, the evidence leaves it doubtful whether or not he recognized Booth under his disguise on the night he set his broken leg, and therefore whether he may have been an accessory after the fact or not; but the testimony of the informer Weichman, by which chiefly if not solely the prosecution sought to implicate the doctor in the conspiracy to murder, was greatly damaged, if not completely broken down, by the proof on the part of the defense that Dr. Mudd had not been in Washington from November or December, 1864, until after the assassination.

III. As to Payne, his guilt of the assault on Seward in complicity with Booth was clear, and confessed by himself. He was but twenty years of age, of weak mind, entirely dominated by the superior intellect and will of Booth. He claimed he acted under the command of his captain. He was so stolidly indifferent during the trial as to raise suspicion of his sanity, and he repeatedly expressed his wish for the termination of the trial so that he might cease to live.

IV. As to the boy Herold, it was manifest that, as the mere tool and puppet of Booth, he was acquainted beforehand with the design of his master to kill the President, but there is no evidence that he aided or abetted Booth in the actual assassination in any way except to participate in his flight after he had got out of Washington.

V. As to Atzerodt, for whom there appears to have been no pity or sign of relenting, it is nevertheless a fact, that the testimony to his lying in wait for Andrew Johnson is so feeble as to be almost farcical. The poor German was a coward and never went near Johnson. There is no circumstance in the evidence inconsistent with his own confession, that he was in the plot to capture, knew nothing of the design to murder until 8 o'clock on the evening of the 14th, and then refused to enact the part assigned him by Booth.

Indeed, it would appear as if the Commission, by a sort of proleptic vision of the future course of the President in his desperate struggle with the Congress, in grim irony actually hung Atzerodt because he did *not* kill Andrew Johnson.

VI. And as to Mrs. Surratt, the only witnesses of importance against her are Weichman and Lloyd. Without their testimony the case for the prosecution could not stand for a moment. Weichman, a boarder and intimate in her house, the college chum of her son, and, equally with him, the associate of Payne, Atzerodt, Herold and Booth, who, frightened almost to death at the outlook, was swearing, under a desperate strain, to clear his own skirts from the conspiracy and thus save his threatened neck: Weichman's testimony before the Commission, even at such a pass, is for some reason quite vague and indefinite, and only becomes deadly when supplemented by Lloyd's. This man Lloyd it was who, in fact, furnished the only bit of evidence directly connecting Mrs. Surratt with the crime. He testifies to two conversations he had with her – one on the 11th and the other on the 14th of April – when she alluded to the weapons left weeks before at the hotel at Surrattsville owned by her and kept by Lloyd – on the 11th, that the "shooting-irons" would be wanted soon; on the 14th, that they would be called for that night. Lloyd, himself, however, admits, and it is otherwise clearly shown, that on the 14th he was so drunk as hardly to be able to stand up. Lloyd, also, was deeply implicated in the conspiracy to capture if not to assassinate. He had aided the fugitive assassins to escape, had kept their weapons hidden in his house, and he had, for two days after his arrest, denied all knowledge of Booth and Herold's stopping at his hotel at midnight after the murder. He had been placed in solitary confinement and threatened with death. His nervous system, undermined by debauchery, gave way; his terrors were startling to witness and drove him well-nigh mad, and, at last, in a moment of distraction, he turned against Mrs. Surratt and her son. Like Weichman's, his, also, was the frenzied effort of a terror-stricken wretch to avoid impending death by pushing someone forward to take his place. Reverdy Johnson, at the close of his plea to the jurisdiction of the court, let fall the following words, no less weighty for their truth than their force:

This conclusion in regard to these witnesses must be, in the minds of the Court, and is certainly strongly impressed upon my own, that, if the facts which they themselves state as to their connection and intimacy with Booth and Payne are true, their knowledge of the purpose to commit the crimes and their participation in them, is much more satisfactorily established than the alleged knowledge and participation of Mrs. Surratt.

Moreover, the testimony of both these witnesses, suborned as they were alike by their terrors and their hopes, is perfectly reconcilable with the alternative hypothesis, either that the woman in what she did was an innocent dupe of the fascinating actor, or that she was unaware of the sudden transformation of the long-pending plot to capture, of which she might have been a tacit well-wisher, into an extemporaneous plot to kill.

Much stress was laid by Mr. Bingham on her solemn denial of any prior acquaintance with Payne when confronted with him on the night of her arrest. But it is more than probable that the non-recognition was unsimulated, because of the disguise and pitiable plight of the desperado, who had been hidden in the mud of the suburbs three days and three nights, and, also, because the non-recognition was shared with her by the other ladies of the house. Besides, that a woman, caught in the toils in which Booth and her own son had unwittingly involved her, under the terror of recent arrest and imminent imprisonment, should have shrunk from any acknowledgment of this midnight intruder, even to the extent of falsehood, certainly is in no wise incompatible with innocence.

These are the only circumstances by which Mrs. Surratt is brought nearer than conjectural connection with the assassination, and the force of these is greatly weakened by the testimony in her defense.

It is neither necessary, nor relevant to this exposition, to enter into a lengthy discussion upon the *pros* and *cons* of her case. Her innocence has been demonstrated in a more decisive manner by subsequent events, and stands tacitly admitted by the acts of the officers of the government. Few impartial hearers would have said then, and no impartial readers will say now, that the testimony against her is so strong as to render her innocence a mere fanciful or even an improbable hypothesis. No one can say that a jury, to a trial by which she was entitled under the Constitution, would have pronounced her guilty, and every one will admit that had her sentence been commuted to imprisonment for life, as five of her judges recommended, she would have been pardoned with Arnold, Spangler and Mudd, and might have been living with her daughter to-day. The circumstances of the whole tragedy warrant the assertion that, had John H. Surratt been caught as were the other prisoners, he, and not she, would have been put upon trial; he, and not she, would have been condemned to death; he, and not she, would have died by the rope. If he was innocent, then much more was she. Mary E. Surratt, I repeat, suffered the death of shame, not for any guilt of her own, but as a vicarious sacrifice for the presumed guilt of her fugitive son.

PART II:
THE VINDICATION

CHAPTER ELEVEN
Setting Aside the Verdict

When the President of the United States, the Secretary of War, the Military Commission, the Judge-Advocates, and the Executioner-General had buried the woman against whose life the whole military power of the Government, fresh from its triumph over a gigantic Rebellion, had been levelled – buried her broken body deep beneath the soil of the prison-yard, in close contact with the bodies of confessed felons; flattened the earth over her grave, replaced the pavement of stone, locked the door of entrance to the charnel-house and placed the key in the keeping of the stern Secretary – they may have imagined that the iniquity of the whole proceeding was hidden forever.

But, *horribile dictu!* the ghost of Mary E. Surratt would not down. It troubled the breast of the witness Weichman. It haunted the precincts of the Bureau of Military Justice. It pursued Bingham into the House of Representatives. It blanched the laurels of the great War Minister. Politics, history and the very vicissitudes of human events seemed subservient to the vindication of this humble victim.

Hardly had the delivery of the prisons of Washington, which followed the close of the trial, taken place, before the man who, as he himself swore, always had been treated as a son by the woman he betrayed, began to make advances to her sorrowing friends. He pretended to make confession of his perjury. He told a friend that his testimony would have been very much more favorable had it not been dictated to him by the officers who had him in charge; that the meeting of Lloyd and Mrs. Surratt was accidental, as she and he (Weichman) had already started for home before Lloyd returned, and only turned back because the buggy was discovered to be broken. The traitor soon discovered that he made no headway by such disclosures, but only met with a sterner repulse and a deeper loathing. His troubled soul then turned to another quarter. It has been stated that his testimony on the trial was somewhat indefinite and inconclusive. Complaints had been uttered by the officers conducting the prosecution. It was proved upon a subsequent occasion that one of these officers had actually threatened the witness that he would hang as an accomplice in the assassination did he not make his evidence more satisfactory. It appeared, also, that the Secretary of War had promised to protect and take care of him. Driven back by Mrs. Surratt's friends from his attempt at propitiation, Weichman resolved that he would yet earn his reward by retouching his former testimony so as to make it more definite and telling. He saw, at last, that to save himself from everlasting ignominy he must, as far as in him lay, make sure of the guilt of his victim. Actuated by these or similar motives, he, on the 11th day of August, 1865, wrote out, and swore to, a statement in which he, by a suspicious exercise of memory, detailed conversations with Mrs. Surratt and significant incidents, all pointing to complicity with Booth, no mention of which had been made on the trial, and which this candid witness stated *"had come to my* (his) *recollection since the rendition of my* (his) *testimony."*

This affidavit, containing (if true) more evidence of the guilt of Mrs. Surratt than his whole testimony on the trial, but, on the other hand, drawn up to suit himself without fear of cross-examination – he transmitted to Colonel Burnett, who, as though he, too, distrusted the sufficiency of the evidence against the dead woman as it had been actually given on the trial, was careful to append the *ex parte* statement to the published report.

Weichman, at length, gets his reward in the shape of a clerkship in the Custom House at Philadelphia.

But the final breaking down of the fabric of testimony against the leaders of the Rebellion, as instigators of the assassination, threw consternation into the Bureau of Military Justice and the Cabinet. Jefferson Davis was still confined in Fort Monroe, and two companies of United States soldiers, who had fought and shed each other's blood in their eagerness to be the first to seize the fugitive, were already quarreling over the $100,000 reward for his arrest as an accomplice of Booth. Clement C. Clay, for whose arrest $25,000 reward had been offered, as another accomplice, was also still in the hands of the authorities. Jacob Thompson, George N. Sanders and Beverly Tucker, for the arrest of each of whom $25,000 had been offered, were still at large. Every one of these men, it should be borne in mind, had been pronounced guilty by the military board which had condemned Mrs. Surratt. John H. Surratt, her son, for whose capture an enormous reward had been offered both by the Government and by the City of Washington, and whom the Military Commission had condemned as the go-between of the President of the Confederacy and his agents in Canada in the instigation of the murderous conspiracy, and also as the active aider and abettor of both Booth and Payne in the perpetration of their bloody crimes; he, too, had so far eluded all efforts to find even his whereabouts. It is only fair to presume that the astute lawyers connected with the Bureau of Military Justice must have had serious misgivings from the first, concerning the testimony of the spies, Montgomery, Conover and others, going to implicate Davis and the Canadian Rebels in the assassination. Such testimony was hearsay or secondary evidence at best; and they could have cherished no hope that such loose talk and the fragmentary repetition of letters heard read would ever be allowed to pass muster by an impartial judge in a civil court. And they had reason to believe that public opinion would not tolerate the experiment of another military commission. As early as July, 1865, an attempt was made to buy the papers of Jacob Thompson, among which it was supposed were the criminatory letters of Davis; and

Attorney-General Speed was dispatched with $10,000 government money to effect the purchase. William C. Cleary, for whom $10,000 reward had been offered as one of the conspirators, and who had just been found guilty by the Military Commission, was to deliver the letters and receive the money. Speed met Cleary at the Clifton House, but the latter, in the meanwhile, had seen in a newspaper a portion of the testimony before the Military Commission implicating him, and he utterly refused to give up the papers, as he had to rely upon them, as he said, to vindicate himself. The shadows thus began to darken over the credibility of the corps of spies that the Bureau had employed. Indictments for perjury against Montgomery, Conover and other paid witnesses began to be talked of. Friends, and enemies as well, of the imprisoned ex-President began to clamor for his trial or release. Even the implicated agents in Canada showed a bold front, and professed a willingness to meet the terrible charge if guaranteed a trial by jury. A jury! A jury of twelve men! Trial by jury! If there was anything that could shake the souls of the members of the Bureau of Military Justice, it was to hear of trial by jury. It was a damnable institution. It impeded justice. It screened the guilty. It was beyond control. It could not be relied on to convict. And yet it was to this tribunal they foresaw they must come.

In September, 1865, embarrassing news arrived at the Department of State. The consul at Liverpool informed the American Minister at London that John H. Surratt was in England and could be extradited at any time. Here was the villain who was, with Booth, the prime mover of the conspiracy and the active accomplice of Booth and Payne in their work of blood. At least, so the Military Commission found, who hung his mother in his stead. And yet the United States Government informed Mr. Adams, and Mr. Adams so informed the consul, that the Government did not intend to prosecute. On the 24th of November ensuing, the War Department, by general order, revoked the "rewards offered for the arrest of Jacob Thompson, Beverly Tucker, George N. Sanders, William S. Cleary and John H. Surratt." Where now was the redoubtable Bingham who, over and over again, had assured the Commission he guided of the unmistakable guilt of all these persons? The whole theory of the Secretary of War, which he had preconceived in the midst of the panic following the assassination, that the murder of the President was the outcome of a deep-laid and widespread conspiracy, of which Jefferson Davis was the head and Booth and Payne the bloody hands – this theory, which the Bureau of Military Justice, aided by Baker and his detectives, had so sedulously labored to establish, and which Judge Bingham had so persistently pressed upon the nine military men who composed the Court, to the exclusion of any such hypothesis as a plot to capture – this preconceived theory all at once fell to the ground. The perjured spies, who had been the willing and paid tools to build it up, were about to be unmasked and their poisoned fangs drawn. After no great interval, Conover was, in fact, convicted of perjury in another case, and sentenced to imprisonment in the Albany penitentiary. The whole prosecution of the so-called conspirators, from its inception to its tragic close, turned out to have been founded on an enormous blunder. The findings of the Commission were falsified. Whatever the guilt of the doomed victims, they were not guilty of the crime of which they were convicted. The terrible conspiracy, stretching from Richmond to Canada, and from Canada back to Washington, involving statesmen and generals, and crowning the wickedness of rebellion with the Medusa-head of assassination, shrank into the comparatively commonplace and isolated offense of the murder of Lincoln and the assault upon Seward, suddenly concocted by Booth, on the afternoon of the 14th of April, in wild despair over the collapse of the Rebellion. In such a predicament, the hanging of Mrs. Surratt could not have been a pleasing reminiscence to the Secretary of War, to Judge-Advocate Holt, or to the hangers-on of the Bureau of Military Justice. At such a moment they certainly had no use for her son John.

On the 12th of November, Preston King, who held one side of the door of the White House while the daughter of Mrs. Surratt pleaded for admission, walked off a ferry-boat into the Hudson River, with two bags of shot in the pockets of his overcoat, and was seen no more. This event might have passed as a startling coincidence, to be interpreted according to the feelings of the hearer, had it not been followed by the suicide of Senator James S. Lane, who held the other side of the door, and who, on the 11th day of July, 1866, blew his brains out on the plains of Kansas. That these two men had together stood between the President and the filial suppliant for mercy, in a case of life and death, and that, then, within a year, both had perished by their own hands, aroused whispers in the air, caused a holding of the breath and a listening, as if to catch the faint but increasing cry of innocent blood, coming up from the ground.

When the Congress met in December, 1865, the leaders of the dominant party were in a fierce and bitter humor. The Rebellion had been suppressed, the South subjugated and its chiefs captured, yet no one – not even the arch-traitor Davis – had been hung. And, more deeply exasperating still, the man they had elected Vice-President, and who had thus succeeded the martyred Lincoln, upon whom their hopes had been fixed to make treason odious, to hang the leaders higher than Haman, and to set aside the humane policy of reconstruction his predecessor had already outlined and substitute a more radical and retributive method – this man, whose precious life had been providentially spared from the pistol of the assassin to be the Moses of the colored people, and for harboring any such blasphemous purpose as lying in wait for him, a Court, appointed by himself and whose sentence he himself had approved, had hung a bewildered German – why this man had already shown himself a renegade, was bent on a general amnesty, appeared to have forgotten the assassination, was already hobnobbing with Southern traitors, and was attempting to carry out a policy of reconstruction in the South, the result of which could be nothing less than the dethronement of the party who had brought the war for the Union to a triumphant end. These men resolved that such treachery should be balked at whatever cost. Ignorant as yet of the tainted character and of the break-down of the evidence adduced to show Confederate complicity in the assassination, the House of Representatives passed resolutions calling for trial of Jefferson Davis for treason and for the other crimes with which he was charged; the ill-starred Bingham, once again in the House, insisting that the Confederate Chief should be put upon trial before a military tribunal for the same offense of which his former court had found him guilty in his absence. The House appointed a committee to investigate the complicity of Davis and others in the assassination, and in July, 1866, through its chairman, Mr. Boutwell, made a report, followed by a resolution, "that it is the duty of the executive department of the Government to proceed with the investigation of the facts connected with the assassination of the late President without unnecessary delay, that Jefferson Davis and others named in the proclamation of President Johnson of May 2d, 1865, may be put upon trial," which was adopted *nem. con.* In this action, little as they recked, these radical politicians were the unconscious tools of that Nemesis which stalks after lawlessness and triumphant crime. This resolution, and the news that John H. Surratt had been betrayed by one of his comrades in the Papal Zouaves into the hands of the Roman authorities, who had detained him to await the order of the American Government, and that the prisoner had escaped from his guard and fled to Malta, forced the Department of War to revoke the order of November, 1865, withdrawing the reward for the arrest of the fugitive.

Meanwhile the great contest over the reconstruction of the South waxed fiercer and fiercer. Congress, during this session, became farther and farther alienated from the President, so that when that body met in December, 1866, the reckless majority in both Houses united in the resolve to get rid of Andrew Johnson, not indeed by the bloody method employed by Booth, but by the no less efficient, though more insidious and less bold, expedient of impeachment by the House and conviction by the Senate. No sooner had Congress convened than Mr. Boutwell made an attack upon the Executive for its dilatory action in the arrest of John H. Surratt, stating that he had reason to believe that the Government knew where the assassin was the May before. A committee appointed to investigate the matter made a report just at the close of the session obliquely censuring the Executive Department for its lack of diligence in effecting the arrest. On January 7th, 1867, the famous Ashley introduced his resolutions impeaching Andrew Johnson. The Judiciary Committee, to which they were referred, took testimony during the winter and made a report at the close of the session that it was unable to complete the investigation, and handed it over to the Fortieth Congress. That Congress met immediately at the close of the Thirty-ninth, and the testimony already taken was referred to the Judiciary Committee of its House, which proceeded with the matter during the spring and summer, and in November, 1867, after the recess; with the final result of a failure to pass the resolution of impeachment reported by a bare majority of the committee.

In process of this investigation all sorts of accusations and charges were made against the President. His enemies now employed the very same weapons against him which had been employed to convict the alleged assassins of his predecessor and the alleged conspirators against his own life. General Baker and his detectives, Conover and his allies, appear once more upon the scene. They actually invaded the privileged quarters of the White House and stationed spies in the very private apartments of the President. This time, however, they are ready to swear, and in fact do swear, not to having seen letters from Jefferson Davis to his agents in Canada advising assassination, but letters from Andrew Johnson to Davis squinting in that direction. They actually charged the President with being an accomplice in the assassination of Abraham Lincoln. Forgetting that a human being had been hung for lying in wait to kill Andrew Johnson as a part of a general conspiracy to murder the heads of the Government, these desperate men propose to impeach the President for being an accomplice in his own attempted murder. Ashley openly denounced him, in the House of Representatives on the 7th of March, 1867, as "the man who came into the Presidency through the door of assassination," and alluded to the "dark suspicion which crept over the minds of men as to his complicity in the assassination plot," and "the mysterious connection between death and treachery which this

this case presents." Ashley had private interviews in the jail with Conover and Cleaver, who were confined there for their crimes, and they assured him of the guilt of Andrew Johnson. They furnished him with memoranda and letters purporting to show that Andrew Johnson and Booth were in communication with each other before the murder of Lincoln, and that Booth had said before his death that if Andrew Johnson dared go back on him he would have him hung higher than Haman. To such preposterous stuff, from professional perjurers, did the zealous Ashley seriously incline.

It was during this investigation that the evidence given by Secretaries Seward and Stanton and by Attorney-Generals Speed and Stansbery, demonstrated the utter futility of an attempt to establish complicity in the assassination on the part of Davis, Thompson and the rest, by witnesses who had been shown, in other cases, to be unworthy of a moment's belief.

While the impeachers were in the very act of pursuing the President as an accomplice in the murder of Abraham Lincoln, while the mighty Bingham, who had so eloquently defended President Johnson before the Military Commission against the charge of usurpation of power, and so bitterly denounced Jefferson Davis for alluding to Johnson as "The Beast," now, with a complete change of tune, was clamoring for the impeachment of "his beloved Commander-in-Chief" – Jefferson Davis, himself, is brought, by direction of the Secretary of War, in obedience to a writ of habeas corpus, before the United States Court at Richmond; there, without a word of remonstrance, transferred to the custody of the civil authority; and forthwith discharged on bail, Horace Greeley, who had never seen him before, becoming one of his bondsmen. Since that day in May, 1867, no attempt has ever been made to call the ex-President of the Southern Confederacy to account as one of the conspirators in the murder of Lincoln. Clay had been let go on parole as long before as April 19th, 1866; his property was restored to him in February, 1867; and proceedings under an indictment found against him for treason and conspiracy, indefinitely suspended on the 26th of March of the same year. Thompson and Sanders and Tucker returned to their country and appeared unmolested amongst us. Jefferson Davis died recently full of years and honors. At the death of Thompson, the flags of the Interior Department were lowered half-mast. Tucker was appointed to office not long ago by President Harrison. And all this, notwithstanding the Judge-Advocate had assured the Military Commission that the guilt of these men was as clear as the guilt of Booth or of Surratt, notwithstanding the Military Commission under his guidance so found, and, had these men been present before that tribunal, would doubtless have hung them on the same scaffold with Mrs. Surratt.

It was during this same investigation, that the diary of Booth, which had been so carefully concealed by the War Department and the Bureau of Military Justice from the Military Commission, was unearthed. Its publication produced a profound sensation, as it made clear the reality of a plan to capture the President; a plan, which had been blasted by the collapse of the Rebellion and, only at the last moment and without consultation, arbitrarily superseded by a hurried resolution to kill. When produced by Judge Holt before the committee, its mutilated condition gave rise to a terrible suspicion. Holt, himself, and Stanton were confident the book was in the same condition as when they first saw it. Colonel Conger, also, though not positive, thought it was unchanged since he took it from the dead body of Booth. But, to the great wonder of everybody, the distinguished detective, General Baker, testified, and stuck to it with emphasis when recalled, that, when he first examined the diary before it was lodged with the Secretary of War, there were no leaves missing and no stubs, although the diary, as exhibited to the committee, showed by means of the stubs remaining that sixteen or twenty leaves had been cut or torn out. The disclosures made by the production of the diary, together with the fact of its suppression, stirred the soul of General Butler; and, in this way, it came about that the ghost of Mrs. Surratt stalked one day into the House of Representatives. Judge Bingham, in his rollicking way, was upbraiding General Butler for having voted for Jefferson Davis fifty times as his candidate for

President, and slurring his war record by calling him "the hero of Fort Fisher;" when, suddenly, at the petrific retort of his adversary that "the only victim of the gentleman's prowess was an innocent woman hung upon the scaffold!" the spectre stood before him, forcing, as from "white lips and chattering teeth," the exclamation of Macbeth: "Thou canst not say I did it!"

"Look to the true and brave and honorable men who found the facts upon their oaths and pronounced the judgment!" he retorted, clutching at the self-soothing sophistry of the murderer of Banquo, ignoring the fact that he himself was a part of the tribunal and virtually dictated the judgment.

Another discovery was made by the Judiciary Committee in the "Article" which, as recorded in his diary, Booth had left behind him for publication in the *National Intelligencer*. John Matthews, a fellow actor and an intimate friend of the assassin, testified that on the afternoon of the 14th of April Booth had met him in the street and left with him a letter directed to that newspaper, to be delivered in the morning. The witness was on the stage of the theatre that night at the time the fatal shot was fired, and, in the confusion that followed, he called to mind the communication. Hurrying to his lodgings he opened the envelope, read the letter, and, fearing to be compromised by the possession of such a document, burnt it up. The substance of the letter, as near as Matthews could recollect, was that for a long time he (Booth) had devoted his money, time and energies to the accomplishment of an end, but had been baffled. "The moment has at length arrived when my plans must be changed. The world may censure me for what I do; but I am sure that posterity will justify me." And the communication was signed (all the names being in the hand-writing of Booth): "Men who love their country better than gold or life. J. W. Booth – Payne – Atzerodt – Herold."

The significance of this piece of testimony was negative. The name of Surratt was not there.

One suggestive circumstance was called out in the testimony of Secretary Seward and General Eckert. It appeared that Payne before his trial had talked with General Eckert about his motives and movements in the assault upon the disabled Secretary of State, the particulars of which conversation Eckert had related to Seward, after the recovery of the latter from his wound, and had promised to reduce to writing. Among other things, Payne had said that he and Booth were in the grounds in front of the White House on the night of Tuesday, the 11th of April, when Abraham Lincoln made his speech of congratulation on the fall of Richmond and the surrender of Lee; and that on that occasion Booth tried to persuade him to shoot the President as he stood in the window, but that he would take no such risk; and that Booth, turning away, remarked, "That is the last speech he will ever make."

Such an incident is consistent only with the theory that the assassination plot was concocted at the last moment as a forlorn hope, and that, if there had been any conspiracy, it was a conspiracy to capture. It is easy to see why the Bureau of Military Justice suppressed this testimony also, because, although it bears hard upon Payne himself, and Herold, and possibly John Surratt, it renders it highly improbable that Mrs. Surratt was aware of any design to kill.

Even such a fragmentary review, as the foregoing, of the public history of the two years succeeding the execution – which any reader may complete, as well as test, for himself by referring to the *Congressional Globe* of that period, to the printed reports of the Committee, and to the leading newspapers of the day – is sufficient to indicate how the general tendency of events, and every event in its place, appear to have conspired to the accomplishment of one result – the setting aside, in the public mind, of the verdict of the Military Commission in the case of Mrs. Surratt.

This was not done by a direct assault upon that tribunal, or upon its mode of procedure; not even upon the character of the witnesses against the particular culprit, nor upon the weakness of the case made against her. These points of attack were all passed by, and the verdict was taken on the flank.

The condemnation of the woman was subverted by the *wind*, so to speak, of passing events.

The irrepressible conflict between the President and the

Congress; the consequent schism in the very ranks of the triumphant conquerors; the insane charge against Andrew Johnson of complicity in a conspiracy against his own life, supported by the incredible statements of the very witnesses who were responsible for the charge of complicity against Jefferson Davis and others; the final and complete exposure of the fiction of a conspiracy to assassinate, either by the Confederate authorities, or anybody else; and the true, historical character of the assassination of Abraham Lincoln – all combined to shake the edifice of guilt, which the Bureau of Military Justice had so carefully built up around their helpless victim, upon such an aerial foundation. Whilst the gradual abatement of that furious uncharitableness, which in the hey-day of the war could find nothing not damnable in the Southern people, and no secessionist who was not morally capable either of murder or of perjury in its defense or concealment, was, surely but imperceptibly, clearing up the general atmosphere of public opinion, and thus preparing for the cordial reception of such a measure of retributive justice, as Time, with his sure revenges, was daily disclosing to be more and more inevitable.

The Milligan decision dissipated the technical jurisdiction of the Commission. But lawyers could still distinguish, and the hyperloyal could still maintain the essential rightfulness of the verdict.

But the explosion of the great assassination conspiracy; the *nol-pros.* of the awful charge against Jefferson Davis, Clement C. Clay, Jacob Thompson, and their followers – a crime, which, if capable of proof, no government on earth would have dared to condone – discredited forever the judgment of the Military Commission, reopened wide all questions of testimony, of character, of guilt or innocence, and summoned the silent and dishonored dead to a new and benignant trial.

CHAPTER TWELVE
Reversal Upon the Merits

  The new trial was in fact at hand. In the summer of the year 1867, the interest excited by the investigation of the Judiciary Committee of the House of Representatives, referred to in the last chapter, suddenly became merged into the intenser and more widespread interest excited by the trial of John H. Surratt in the Criminal Court of the District of Columbia.

  Surratt, after escaping from his captors in Italy by leaping down a precipice, fled to Malta and thence to Alexandria, where, on the 21st of December, 1866, he was recaptured and taken on board the United States vessel *Swatara*. In this vessel, bound hand and foot, the prisoner arrived at Washington on the 21st of February following. Thus the radicals in Congress, impelled by their growing enmity to the President over the reconstruction contest, by scattering abroad sinister intimations that the cau
se of his remissness in bringing to punishment the accomplices of the convicted assassins was fear for himself of a full investigation of the assassination, succeeded at last in forcing the Executive Department, apprehensive, as it had good reason to be, of the shadows which any future trial in the civil courts was likely to reflect back upon the Military Commission, and aware of the breaking down of the case against the Canadian confederates and

Jefferson Davis, face to face with the necessity of ratifying the conviction of the mother by securing the conviction of the son. On the one hand, the radicals, in blind ignorance of the true inwardness of affairs, clamored for the trial, in the hope that the guilt of the prisoner's supposed accomplices, Davis and Company, and possibly of the President himself, might be detected. On the other hand, the administration, now that the man had been forced upon its hands, knowing the futility of the hope of its enemies, pushed on the trial in the hope that, with its powerful appliances, a result could be obtained which would vindicate the verdict of the Military Commission. No one on either side, however, so much as dreamed of renewing the iniquity of a trial by court-martial. Amid the silence of the Holts and the Binghams and the Stantons, Surratt was duly indicted by a grand jury for the murder of "one Abraham Lincoln," and for conspiring with Booth, Payne, Atzerodt, Herold and Mary E. Surratt to murder "one Abraham Lincoln," which conspiracy was executed by Booth. There was no averment about the traitorous conspiracy to murder the heads of Government, in aid of the Rebellion; nor were the names of Dr. Mudd, O'Laughlin, Arnold or Spangler, then undergoing punishment on the Dry Tortugas, inserted as parties to the conspiracy; nor was any mention made of Seward or Johnson or Grant, as among the contemplated victims. All was precise and perspicacious, as is required in pleadings in the civil courts. The loose, vague, indefinite and impalpable charges permissible, seemingly, on military trials, gave place to plain and simple allegations, such as an accused person might reasonably be expected to be able to meet. On Monday, June 10, 1867, while the investigation before the Judiciary Committee of the House was still going on, while the sensation produced by the sight of Booth's diary and by Matthews' disclosures was still fresh, while the echoes of the encounter of Bingham and Butler still lingered in the air, the momentous trial came on. Great and unprecedented preparations had been made by the prosecution. Again the country was ransacked for witnesses, as in the palmy days of Baker and his men. Again the Montgomeries and other Canada spies haunted the precincts of the District Attorney's office, willing as ever to swear to anything necessary to make out the case for the prosecution. Even the voice of Conover was heard, *de profundis clamavi*, from his dungeon cell. The Bureau of Military Justice started into active life, and Holt and his satellites bestirred themselves as though fully conscious of the impending crisis. Indeed, every one of these officials, from the President and the Secretary of War down to the meanest informer and hired hangman, who had had anything to do with the trial and execution of Mary E. Surratt, felt as if he, too, was to be put on trial in the trial of her son. A Court recognized in, and drawing its life and jurisdiction from, the Constitution was to act as a court of appeal to review the process and judgment of that extra-constitutional tribunal, which had, summarily and without legal warrant, put a free American woman to a felon's death. A Daniel in the shape of a jury – a common law jury – a jury of civilians – unadorned by sword, epaulette or plume – a jury guaranteed by the Bill of Rights – a Daniel had come to judgment! The Shylocks of the days of arbitrary power dropped their sharpened knives and ejaculated, "Is that the law?"

Great, assuredly, must have been the flurry of the once omnipotent Bureau, when it was ascertained that the tribunal before which it must come could not be "organized to convict;" that there could be no soldiery around the Court, no shackles on the prisoners or the witnesses for the defense, no prosecuting officers in the jury room. Everything must be done decently and in order, with the same calm dignity, unruffled composure, the same presumption of the innocence of the accused, as though the murdered man had been the humblest citizen of the land. One great advantage, however, the prosecution managed to secure. A Judge was selected to preside whom they could rely on, as "organized to convict." But this was the sole reminiscence of the unbridled reign of the military only two years before. A jury of twelve intelligent men, some of them the best citizens of the District, was speedily obtained to the evident satisfaction of both the people and the prisoner – and the succeeding Monday, the 17th, the struggle began.

As we have given the names of the members of the Court which tried the mother, we may be pardoned for giving the names of the jurors who tried the son. Although there were no major-generals among them, they are entitled to the honor of being within, and not without, the ægis of the Constitution.

The jurors were W.B. Todd, Robert Ball, J. Russell Barr, Thomas Berry, George A. Bohrer, C.G. Schneider, James Y. Davis, Columbus Alexander, William McLean, Benjamin Morsell, B. E. Gittings, W.W. Birth.

They were thus spoken of by the District Attorney:

> It is a matter of mutual congratulation that a jury has been selected agreeable to both parties; the representatives of the wealth, the intelligence, and the commercial and business character of this community; gentlemen against whose character there cannot be a whisper of suspicion. I would trust you with my life and my honor; and I will trust you with the honor of my country.

The scene which the court-room presented, when the Assistant District Attorney arose to open the case for the United States, afforded a speaking contrast to the scene presented at the opening of the Military Commission. The Court was not held in a prison, and there was an entire absence of the insignia of war. The doors of the court-room were wide open to the entrance of the public, not locked up in sullen suspicion, and the keys in the hands of the prosecuting officer. The counsel for the prisoner confronted the jury and the witness-stand upon an equal line with the counsel for the United States; and there was neither heard, seen, nor surmised, in the words or bearing of Edwards Pierrepont, the leading counsel for the prosecution, any of the insolence and supercilious condescension shown in the words and bearing of John A. Bingham.

As the prisoner entered the court and advanced to the bar, no clank of fetters jarred upon the ear; and, as he sat at his ease by the side of his counsel, like a man presumed to be innocent, the recollection of that wan group of culprits, loaded down with iron, as they crouched before their imperious doomsmen, must have aroused a righteous wrath over the barbarous procedure of the military, in comparison with the benign rules of the civil, tribunals. The atmosphere surrounding the court and the trial seemed, also, to be free from passion and prejudice, when contrasted with the tremendous excitement and the thirst for blood, which permeated the surroundings of the Military Commission. Although the Bureau of Military Justice had busied itself in the prosecution, and thrust its aid on the office of the District Attorney; although the whole weight of the federal administration was thrown in the same direction to vindicate, if possible, the signature of the President to the death warrant of the victims of his military court; and notwithstanding the presence upon the bench of a judge "organized to convict:" still, so repellant to partial passion were the precincts of what might fitly be styled a temple of justice, a neutral spectator might feel reliance that in that chamber innocence was safe.

But there was one sentiment hovering over the trial and dwelling in all bosoms, which clothed the proceedings with a peculiar awfulness. All felt that the dead mother was on trial with the living son. She had been executed two years before for the same crime with which he was now charged. And, as he stood in the flesh, with upraised hand, looking at the jury which held his life in its hands, it required no great effort of fancy to body forth the image of his mother, standing beside him, murmuring from shadowy lips the plea of not guilty, amid the feeble repetitions of which, to her priest, she had died upon the scaffold. To convict her son, now, by the unanimous verdict of twelve men, and punish him according to law, would go far to condone the unconstitutional trial and illegal execution of the mother. Whereas, on the other hand, the acquittal of her son of the same crime, by the constitutional tribunals of the country, would forever brand the acts of the Military Commission as murder under the forms of military rule. This dread alternative met the prosecution at the threshold of the trial, oppressed them with its increasing weight during its progress, and tarried with them even at its close. It appeared in the indictment, where the name of the mother, as one of the conspirators, was associated with the name of her son. It appeared in the examination of the jurors, when Judge Pierrepont endeavored to extract from them whether they had formed or expressed an opinion as to the guilt or the innocence of the prisoner, not only, but also as to the guilt or the innocence of his mother. It appeared during the taking of testimony, where evidence bearing upon the guilt of Mrs. Surratt alone was admitted at all times as evidence against her son. It appeared in the argument of the District Attorney, when he compares the mother of the prisoner to Herodias and Lucrezia Borgia, and "traces her connection with the crime" and "leaves it to the jury to say whether she was guilty;" where he pleads, like Antony, in behalf of the members of the Military Commission that they were "all honorable men," and were not to be blamed for obeying the orders of the President. It appeared in the arguments of the counsel for the prisoner, when Mr. Merrick taunted the Government that they were pressing for a verdict to "vindicate the fearful action they had committed;" when he appealed to the jury to "deal fairly by this young man," "even if the reputation of Joseph Holt should not have the vindication of innocent blood;" when he invoked the spirit of Mrs. Surratt as a witness for her son, and rebuked the prosecution for objecting to the admission of her dying declaration when they were putting her again on trial though dead; when Mr. Bradley charged that for four weeks and more they had been trying Mrs. Surratt and not her son, and denounced Weichman and Lloyd, avowing that "the proof against her was not sufficient to have hung a dog" and was "rotten to the core." It appeared in the speech of Judge Pierrepont, when he flourished the record of the Military Commission before the jury, and asserted that the recommendation of Mrs. Surratt to mercy was attached to it; in his avowal of his belief in her guilt; in his extolling the jury as a tribunal far more fit for the trial of such crimes than any military court; and in his covert threat that the people would punish the City of Washington by the removal of the Capitol, if the jury, by their verdict, did not come up to the high standard erected for them. And, lastly, it appeared in the charge of the Judge, which is a model of what a one-sided charge ought to be. It opens with the words of the Old Testament: "Whoso sheddeth man's blood, by man shall his blood be shed." Then follows a sneer at the "sentimental philosophers," who were opposed to capital punishment. Then the Court inveighs against some imaginary advocates, who argued that to kill a king was a greater crime than to kill a president; and then casts an imputation upon the integrity of the decision in the Milligan Case, as "predicated upon a misapprehension of historic truth," and that therefore "we could not perhaps have looked for a more rightful deduction," "all loyal hearts" being "unprepared for such an announcement." The Judge, then, holds that the Court will take judicial cognizance that the crime charged was the murder of the President of the United States, and a more heinous offense than the murder of a simple individual. He, then, complacently sets aside the rule of Sir Matthew Hale, implicitly followed since, as he himself admits, by "writers and judges seeming contented with his reasons or indisposed to depart from his principles," as "not very satisfactory to my (the Judge's) mind;" and accordingly he declares that, in felonies of such high grade, as in cases of treason, there can be no accessories before the fact, but all are principals; and, to support this conclusion, he then cites and details at length two cases, apparently overruling Sir Matthew beforehand; (as he says) "reported in that book of highest authority known among Christian nations, decided by a judge from whose decision there can be no appeal and before whose solemn tribunal all judges and jurors will in the great day have their verdict and judgments passed in review." One, the case "of Naboth and Ahab, contained in the 21st chapter of the First Book of Kings," the other, "that of David and Uriah, recorded in the 11th chapter of Second Samuel;" at the end of the statement of which case the Judge remarks, "this judgment of the Lord was not that David was accessory before the fact of this murder, but was guilty as the principal, because he procured the murder to be done. It was a judgment to the effect that he who does an act by another does it himself, whether it be a civil or a criminal act." This extraordinary deliverance closes with an echo of Judge Pierrepont's warning to the jury, to uphold by their verdict the District of Columbia, as a place for "the public servants, commissioned by the people of the nation, to do their work safe and sacred from the presence of unpunished assassins within its borders."

It would be foreign to our purpose, as well as tedious to the reader, to examine in detail the testimony given on this trial. One conclusion – and that is the important thing – is certain. It is true, beyond the shadow of a doubt, that the prosecution made an incomparably stronger case against Surratt than was made against his mother. They had but one culprit at whom to direct their aim, and they made a far more desperate and thorough-going effort to convict, because of the known unreliability of a jury to do what the prosecution might tell them to do without the aid of proof. Before a Military Commission, tossed about by the passions of its members and steered by Judge-Advocates, the accusers could afford to be careless of gaps in their scheme of proof, missing links in the chain of circumstantial evidence. Not so now and here. Vehement affirmation without evidence availed nothing. Curses against treason, traitors, disloyalty, apostrophes to the imperiled Union, tears over the beloved Commander-in-Chief, could fill no void in the testimony. Of course, there was no such outrage against not only the elementary rules of evidence, but against ordinary decent fairness, as an attempt to introduce testimony of the horrors of Libby Prison and Andersonville; but the door looking in that direction was opened as wide as possible by the eager Judge. All the material testimony given upon the "Conspiracy Trial" against Mrs. Surratt, not only, but also against Payne, Herold, Atzerodt, Arnold and O'Laughlin, was reproduced here. The direct testimony on the part of the United States occupied from June 17th to July 5th, and in that period eighty-five witnesses were examined. On the Conspiracy Trial, the direct case consumed the time from May 12th to May 25th, and about one hundred and thirty witnesses were examined against the eight accused persons, not only, but also against the eight accessories, headed by Jefferson Davis, included in the charge, the testimony ranging over the whole Rebellion and including Libby, Andersonville, Canada,

St. Albans, and projected raids on New York, Washington and other cities. Every witness, whose testimony on the former trial had the remotest bearing upon the question of the guilt or innocence of Mrs. Surratt, once more showed his face and retold his story.

Lloyd was there, compelled, despite his superstitious reluctance to speak against a woman now she was dead, to rehearse the tale which his terrors had evolved out of his drunken imagination. This time, however, his sottish memory or failure of memory, his fright at the time of his arrest, his repeated denials of the visit of Booth and Herold, his temptations and bribes to accuse his landlady, were, under the keen cross-examination of the counsel for the prisoner, fully exposed.

Weichman "came also," this time with his story carefully elaborated, touched and retouched here and there, and written down beforehand. He had been engaged for three or four months in aiding the prosecution, had prepared a carefully detailed statement for the use of the Assistant District Attorney, and now openly acknowledged that "his character was at stake" in this trial, and that he "intended to do all he could to help the prosecution." He had conned over and over again the report of his evidence on the Conspiracy Trial, had corrected it to meet objections subsequently made and to eliminate discrepancies and contradictions, and had thus brought its several disjointed parts into some logical sequence; he then had added to it the incidents and conversations disclosed for the first time in the affidavit sent to Colonel Burnett, which was appended to the published report of the trial, to which allusion has been made; and, now, in the final delivery of his deadly charge, coolly averring that his memory was much more distinct now than at the time of the former trial two years ago, he, with a superadded concentrated venom, flavored his narrative with a few damning incidents never heard of before – one, the most poisonous of all, that on the evening of the fatal 14th, while Booth was about his murderous work, Mrs. Surratt was pacing her parlor floor begging her pious boarder "to pray for her intentions." This time, however, the witness did not escape unscathed. When he emerged from the skillful hands of Mr. Bradley, his malicious and sordid *animus* laid bare – his self-contradictions, his studied revisions, his purposeful additions to his testimony, exposed – his intimacy with the conspirators, his terrified repentance, his abject self-surrender and his cowardly eagerness to shift his peril upon the head of his protectress – and then his simulated remorse and his later recantation – all made clear – he was an object of loathing to gentlemen; a stumbling block to the philanthropist; to the indifferent, an enigma; and to the common man, a perpetual provocation to a breach of the peace.

Twelve witnesses testified that they saw John H. Surratt in Washington on the 14th of April, only one of whom had testified to that effect on the other trial. It is curious now to discern how the memory of the witnesses, it may be unconsciously, swerved under pressure toward the mark of identification. The witnesses for the defense established that the prisoner was in Elmira on the afternoon of the 13th, made it more than probable he was there on the 14th, and almost certain he was there on the 15th. The prosecution, under the force of this proof, suddenly conceded his presence in Elmira on the 13th, and then, by the accident of a special train and the testimony of a ferryman whom the notorious Montgomery unearthed in the very crisis of the emergency, contrived with much straining to land him in Washington at 10 o'clock on the morning of the fatal day. Any calm observer, reading the account of the trial now, can see plainly that the truth is, the prisoner had not been in Washington since the 3rd of April.

The production of Booth's diary by the prosecuting officers was forced upon them by the popular indignation over its suppression before the Military Commission; otherwise, it is clear they would not have been guilty of such a mistake in tactics as its introduction as a part of the case for the United States. Its opening sentences – "Until to-day nothing was ever thought of sacrificing to our country's wrongs. For six months we had worked to capture. But our cause being almost lost something decisive and great must be done" – settled the question of a plot to kidnap suddenly given up; and the testimony of Weichman indicated the hour of abandonment.

That every conceivable effort to obtain the conviction of the prisoner was made, and that a most formidable array of circumstances was marshalled against him, compared to which the two disconnected pieces of evidence which were so magnified against his mother seem weak indeed, will be controverted by no sane person. From June 10th to August 7th– nearly two months – the contest went on. On the last-mentioned day, which was Wednesday, Judge Fisher delivered his remarkable charge, and a little before noon the jury retired. At one o'clock in the afternoon of Saturday, the 10th, after a session of three days and three nights, a communication was received from the jury to the effect that they stood as at first, nearly equally divided, that they could not possibly agree, and the health of several of their numbers was becoming seriously impaired. The Court, notwithstanding the protest of the prisoner, discharged the jury, and the prisoner was remanded to jail.

There he did not long remain, however. Every one recognized the futility of another trial. The strength of the proof of the prisoner's presence in Elmira on the day of the assassination wrought a reaction of public opinion in his favor. The administration was glad to escape with less than an unequivocal condemnation. The Bureau of Military Justice was silent. John H. Surratt was quietly let go.

This obscure occurrence, the discharge of John H. Surratt, which caused not a ripple on the surface of human affairs, nevertheless constituted a cardinal event; for it worked a national estoppel. When that young man stepped forth from the threshold of the prison, to which the United States had brought him in irons from Egypt across the Mediterranean and the Atlantic, not to follow his mother to the scaffold and a felon's grave, but to walk the earth a living, free man – the innocence of the mother was finally and forever established by the universal acknowledgment of all fair men. No condemnation of the Military Commission could be so heavy, and at the same time so indubitably final, as the simultaneous conviction arrived at by all men, that if the son had been tried by such a tribunal he would assuredly have been put to death, and that if the mother had been reserved to calmer times and the tribunal guaranteed by the Constitution to every man and woman, she would now have been living with her daughter, instead of lying, strangled to death, beneath the pavement of a prison.

CHAPTER THIRTEEN
The Recommendation to Mercy

The worst was still behind.

It was left to Time to disclose the astounding fact, that all the military machinery of the War Department, its Bureaus, its Court, its Judge-Advocates, its unconstitutional, anti-constitutional and extra-constitutional processes, would not have compassed the death of this helpless woman, had not the prosecutors, in the last extremity, called in the help of Fraud.

It has been narrated in the chronological order of events, how five members of the Military Commission were, in all probability, beguiled into the abdication of their own power of commutation and did, as matter of fact, sign a paper "praying" the President, "if he could find it consistent with his sense of duty to the country," to commute the death sentence of Mrs. Surratt; how that the paper may have been carried to the President by Judge Holt and have been present at the confidential interview when the death warrant was composed; and how that Judge Holt, in drafting the death warrant, went out of his way to so write it out, as in fact, if not by design, to withdraw from the eye of the President, as he signed it, this paper praying him to withhold his signature.

But it should be borne in mind that all this was shrouded in the deepest secrecy. That there had been any hesitation among the members of the Commission in fixing the sentence of Mrs. Surratt – any more than in the cases of Herold, Atzerodt and Payne – much more that it had been found necessary to resort to a petition to the President, was entirely unknown to the public at large. As to what had taken place in the sessions of the Court when the sentences were made up, every member thereof and the three Judge-Advocates were sworn to secrecy; and, outside these officers, the knowledge of the petition was confined to the Secretary of War (possibly the Attorney-General) and one or two subordinates in the War Department. The record of the findings and sentences, to which the petition was attached, was kept from the official reporters, and not a soul outside a close coterie in the War Department was allowed to set eyes on it.

In the recital of the death sentences in the order of the Adjutant-General directing their execution, the sentence of the woman differed in no respect from the three sentences of the men which preceded it. So far as the public eye could discover, there was not a gleam of mercy for the woman in the bosom of the Commission.

It is true, that even before the execution there were rumors that the Court had united in a recommendation to mercy, and it was stated in the newspapers of the 6th and 7th of July that five members of the Commission had signed such a recommendation and the whole Court concurred in it. It is also certain, that almost immediately after the execution the story sprang up that the President had never been allowed to see the recommendation which the Court had addressed to him.

But all these statements remained without corroboration from any authentic source, and could not stand before the indubitable facts of the sentence, its approval by the President, and its summary execution. The single indication that in all these reports the paper is miscalled "a recommendation to mercy" shows of itself that the real nature of the secret was well kept.

In November, 1865, there appeared a volume compiled by Benn Pitman styled "The Recorder to the Commission," claiming to be "An authentic record of the trial of the assassins of the late

President," to which was prefixed a certificate "to its faithfulness and accuracy" by Colonel Burnett, who had been assigned by Judge Holt to superintend the compilation and "made responsible for its strict accuracy." This work, so authenticated, was on its face intended by its compiler to be a complete history "for future use and reference" of the proceedings of the Commission, from the order of the President convening it to the approval of the President of its findings and sentences. It had for frontispiece portraits of the conspirators and a map of portions of Maryland and Virginia showing the route of Booth, and for afterpiece a diagram of the stage of Ford's theatre and a diagram of the streets in its vicinity. Beside matter strictly of record, such as the testimony and the findings and sentences, it included the arguments of all the counsel, the approval of the President, the order changing the place of imprisonment from Albany to the Dry Tortugas, the proceedings under the writ of habeas corpus in the case of Mrs. Surratt; and (in the appendix) the opinion of Attorney-General Speed; army instructions in ten sections; a proclamation of President Lincoln; a poisonous affidavit of Weichman, inclosed in a letter to Colonel Burnett; and an affidavit of Captain Dutton, who took Dr. Mudd to the Dry Tortugas, giving the confessions the Captain swears the Doctor made on the way, sent to General Holt in obedience to his request for such information. Nevertheless, amid all this wealth of illustration, there is not the faintest allusion to any such thing as a recommendation to mercy, in the volume. On the one hand, Pittman may not have seen the paper. His findings and sentences are obviously taken from the order of the Adjutant-General, and not from the original record, as he puts them in the same order, which is not the order of the record. But, if he never saw the paper, it must have been purposely kept from his knowledge, and thus from the knowledge of the public, by some person interested in its suppression. And Colonel Burnett, who had himself attached the paper "at the end" of the record, instead of certifying to the "faithfulness and accuracy" of a compilation omitting it, ought rather to have insisted that so important and interesting a document, about the existence of which so much talk had arisen, be at last given to the world.

On the other hand, if Pitman knew of the paper, he certainly would not have voluntarily left it out of his book for the reason, he himself felt constrained afterwards to assign, that "it formed no part of the proceedings, was not mentioned in open session;" since he had given room to so much matter, not of record, solely for the purpose of adding interest and completeness to his work, and this critical document could add so much to the one and its absence detract so much from the other.

Moreover, in December, the report of the Judge-Advocate-General to the Secretary of War appeared, in which the trial was reviewed, and to which the report to the President, dated July 5th, 1865, was appended. But in both the existence of the petition was ignored.

Whatever may have been the true inwardness of these significant omissions, their inevitable effect was to convince the mass of the people of the non-existence of a recommendation to mercy; and the petition of the five officers might have reposed in silence in the secret archives of the War Department, had it not been for the alienation of the President from the party which had elected him, his gradual gravitation towards his own section, and finally his revolt from the sway of Stanton. During this period, the rumors that the Court had recommended Mrs. Surratt to the clemency of the Executive and that the paper had never reached the Executive, coupled with stories that from the close of the trial to the hour of the execution the President had been kept under confinement and in a state of semi-stupefaction by a band of reckless partisans who were bound there should be no clemency, grew louder and louder. But they were never traceable to any reliable source. In fact, the coolness which had been for a long time growing between Andrew Johnson and Edwin M. Stanton did not break out into an open rupture until as late as the month of March, 1867. The other members of the Cabinet, which Johnson had inherited from Lincoln, who disagreed with Johnson on the question of Reconstruction, Harlan, Dennison and Speed, resigned, on account of that disagreement, in the summer of 1866; but Stanton stayed on. When the Tenure of Office bill was passed by the Congress in February, 1867, the Secretary of War was still so much in accord with the President as to unite with the other members of the reconstructed Cabinet in an emphatic condemnation of the bill as unconstitutional, and to be asked by the President to draft his veto message.

But, on the passage of that Act over the veto, Stanton, thinking his tenure of office secure, at last threw off the double-faced mask he seems to have worn in every Cabinet to which he ever had the honor to belong. From that time he stood alone in the Cabinet, irreconcilable in his hostility to every move of his Chief, in open league with his Chief's active enemies, and determined to remain where he was not wanted and could only act as a hindrance and a spy. In this perilous state of affairs, a secret like that of the petition of the five officers burned towards disclosure. Yet, so far as is at present ascertainable, no authoritative affirmation of the existence of such a paper, on the one hand, and no authoritative denial that it had been presented to the President, on the other, had yet been made.

Upon such an arrangement of combustible material, the trial of John H. Surratt acted like a spark of fire.

On the second day (June 11th, 1867), during the impanelling of the jury, Mr. Pierrepont, the leading counsel for the United States, alluding to the rumors then flying about, took occasion to predict that the Government on that trial would set all these false stories at rest.

Among other things he said:

> It has likewise been circulated through all the public journals that after the former convictions, when an effort was made to go to the President for pardon, men active here at the seat of government prevented any attempt being made or the President being even reached for the purpose of seeing whether he would not exercise clemency; whereas the truth, and the truth of the record which will be presented in this court, is that all this matter was brought before the President and presented to a full Cabinet meeting, where it was thoroughly discussed; and after such dis-

cussion, condemnation and execution received not only the sanction of the President but that of every member of his Cabinet.

The testimony in the case closed, however, and the summing up began, and there had been no attempt at a fulfillment of this prediction.

On Thursday afternoon, August 1st, Mr. Merrick, the junior counsel for the prisoner, then nearing the close of his address, twitted the prosecution with this breach of its promise in these words:

> Where is your record? Why didn't you bring it in? Did you find at the end of the record a recommendation to mercy in the case of Mrs. Surratt that the President never saw? You had the record here in Court.
> Mr. Bradley: And offered it once and withdrew it?
> Mr. Merrick: Yes, sir; offered it and then withdrew it.
> Did you find anything at the close of it that you did not like? Why didn't you put that record in evidence, and let us have it here?

Stung by the necessity of making some answer to this defiant challenge, Mr. Pierrepont on the moment sent for the record. And in response to the summons, Judge-Advocate Holt, who naturally must have followed the prosecution and trial with the most absorbing anxiety, on that very afternoon brought the record "with his own hand," "with his own voice" told its history, in the presence of "three gentlemen," to Mr. Pierrepont, and then left the papers with him.

On the succeeding day, August 2nd, Mr. Bradley, the senior counsel of the prisoner, renewed the attack:

> It was boastfully said in the opening of this case that they would vindicate the conduct of the law officers of the Government engaged in the conspiracy trials. They would produce Booth's diary; they would show that the judgment of the court was sub-

mitted to the Cabinet and fully approved; that no recommendation for mercy for Mrs. Surratt – that no petition for pardon to the Government – had been withheld from the President. Is it so?

The next morning, Saturday, August 3d, Mr. Pierrepont began his address to the jury. Having kept possession of the record since Thursday afternoon, and having been made acquainted with its history by Judge-Advocate Holt in such an impressive manner, he, thus, in his exordium, at last, redeemed the promise of the prosecution:

> The counsel certainly knew when they were talking about that tribunal [i.e. the Military Commission], and when they were thus denouncing it, that President Johnson... ordered it with his own hand, that President Johnson... signed the warrant that directed the execution, that President Johnson... when that record was presented to him, laid it before his Cabinet, and that every single member voted to confirm the sentence, and that the President with his own hand wrote his confirmation of it, and with his own hand signed the warrant. I hold in my hand the original record, and no other man as it appears from that paper ordered it. No other one touched this paper, and when it was suggested by some of the members of the Commission that in consequence of the age and the sex of Mrs. Surratt, it might possibly be well to change her sentence to imprisonment for life, he signed the warrant for her death with the paper right before his eyes – and there it is (handing the paper to Mr. Merrick). My friend can read it for himself.

This is the first appearance in public of the precious record. On Wednesday, July 5th, 1865, Andrew Johnson put his name to the death-warrant written on its back by Judge Holt. And, now, two years after, emerging from its hiding-place, it is flung upon a table in a court-room by the counsel for the United States.

Even now it seems to be destined to a most unsatisfactory publication. For the counsel of the prisoner decline to look at it, because (as Mr. Merrick subsequently explained), "he mistrusted whatever came from the Judge-Advocate-General's office;" because it "had been carefully withheld until all opportunity had passed for taking evidence in relation to it;" and because the official report of the trial contained no recommendation of mercy. The mysterious roll of paper, consequently, lies there unopened, until Judge Holt comes to reclaim it that same afternoon; and that officer is careful, when receiving it back, to repeat over again, before other witnesses, the same history of the document, he had told before to the counsel for the prosecution, and which that counsel had just retold to the jury.

But that had been said and done which must blow away the atmosphere of unwholesome secrecy which had so long enveloped this addendum to the record. The explicit declaration of the counsel for the United States, made in a crowded court-room on so celebrated a trial, with the "identical paper" in his hand, that the President had laid the record before his Cabinet and "every single member voted to confirm the sentence," and that the President had signed the death-warrant with the "suggestion" of commutation "right before his eyes," was immediately published far and wide, and must have been read on Sunday, the 4th, or at latest on Monday, the 5th, by the President himself. And the President was certainly astounded. By a most singular providence, Judge Holt himself, in a letter written to himself, at his request, by his chief clerk, and published by him in 1873 for another purpose, has furnished independent proof that the President was now for the first time startled into sending for the record.

Here is what Chief Clerk Wright says:

> On the 5th day of August, 1867, Mr. Stanton, the Secretary of War, sent for me, and in the presence of General Grant asked me who was in charge of the Bureau in your absence. I informed him Colonel Winthrop. He requested I should send him over to him, which I did. The Colonel returned and asked me for the findings and sentence of the conspiracy trial, telling me he had to take it to the President. On taking the portion of the record referred to from the bundle, I found, from the frequent handling of it, several of the last leaves had torn loose from the rib-

bon fastening, and to secure them I put the eyelet in one corner of it.

The Judge-Advocate-General, though in court on Saturday getting back the record and retelling its history, was absent, it would appear, from his office on Monday, or was considered absent by Stanton, who it also appears was still Secretary of War and in communication with Johnson. It was thought best to employ a deputy to carry the papers to the President. Holt, probably, had no stomach for another "confidential interview," with the identical record in his hand.

Let Andrew Johnson himself tell what followed. The statement is from his published reply to Holt in 1873, and was made with no reference to, and apparently with no recollection of, the foregoing incidents of the John H. Surratt trial:

> Having heard that the petition had been attached to the record, I sent for the papers on the 5th day of August, 1867, with a view of examining, for the first time, the recommendation in the case of Mrs. Surratt.
>
> A careful scrutiny convinced me that it was not with the record when submitted for my approval, and that I had neither before seen nor read it.

It may have been only a coincidence, but on this very day, Monday, August 5th, 1867, and necessarily after the sending for the record, because that was done through the Secretary of War, the following interesting missive was dispatched by the President to that member of his Cabinet:

> Sir: Public considerations of a high character constrain me to say that your resignation as Secretary of War will be accepted.

Stanton immediately replied:

> Public considerations of a high character constrain me not to resign before the next meeting of Congress.

And, on the 12th, he was suspended from office.

But Andrew Johnson was not the only interested personage who read the explicit declaration of Mr. Pierrepont. The statement that every member of the Cabinet voted to confirm the sentence of Mrs. Surratt, with the record, including, of course, the recommendation, before them, must have been read also by William H. Seward, Edwin M. Stanton, Hugh McCulloch, and Gideon Welles, the members of that "full Cabinet" who still remained in office. They surely knew the truth of the statement, if it was true, or its falsity, if it was false. If it was true, is it not perfectly inconceivable that the President, conscious that these four of his confidential advisers had seen the record and voted to deny the petition, would have dared to enact the comedy of sending for the record, and then brazenly assert that the petition had not been attached to it when before him, and that he had neither seen nor read it?

And if he had been guilty of so foolhardy a course of action, now was the time for the Judge-Advocate to fortify the declaration which he had inspired Mr. Pierrepont to make, by appealing to these members of the Cabinet to confront their shameless chief with their united testimony, and forever silence the "atrocious accusation."

From his course of proceeding at a later day, it is not probable that he made any such attempt. At all events, he got no help from Seward, from McCulloch or from Welles. Nay, he got no help to sustain his history of the record, even from Stanton. If help came from that quarter at all, it was to shield him from the awakened wrath of the hood-winked Executive, by drawing the fire upon the head of his department.

But what the Judge-Advocate-General did do, in view of the crisis, is sufficiently apparent. He took immediate measures to retract all that portion of Mr. Pierrepont's declaration of Saturday, which expressed or implied any knowledge on the part of the Cabinet of the disputed paper.

The counsel for the United States had continued his speech to the jury all day Monday, apparently unconscious of the tempes-

The Recommendation to Mercy

tuous effect of his statement of Saturday, and of the predicament in which it had involved his informant. In the evening, he must have had a "confidential interview" with Judge Holt. For, on rising to resume his speech on Tuesday morning, the 6th of August, from no apparent logical cause arising from the course of his argument, he saw fit to recur to the now absent record, and to interpolate the following perfectly insulated and seemingly superfluous piece of information:

> You will recollect, gentlemen, when a call was made several days ago by Mr. Merrick... asking that we should produce the record of the Conspiracy Trial, that I brought the original record here and handed it to counsel. I then stated that as a part of that record was a suggestion made by a part of the Court that tried the conspirators, that, if the President thought it consistent with his public duty, they would suggest, in consideration of the sex and age of one of those condemned, that a change might be made in her sentence to imprisonment for life. I stated that I had been informed that when that record was before the President, and when he signed the warrant of execution, that recommendation was then before him. I want no misunderstanding about that, and I do not intend there shall be any. That is a part of the original record which I here produced in Court. It is in the hand-writing of one of the members of that Court, to wit, General Ekin. The original of that is now in his possession and in the hand-writing of Hon. John A. Bingham. When the counsel called for that record, I sent the afternoon of that day to the Judge-Advocate-General, in whose possession these records are. He brought it to me with his own hand, and told me with his own voice, in the presence of three other gentlemen, that that identical paper, then a part of the record, was before the President when he signed the warrant of execution, and that he had a conversation with the President at that time on the subject. That is my authority. Subsequently to this, having presented it here, the Judge-Advocate-General called to receive it back, and reiterated in the presence of other gentlemen the same thing. That is my knowledge and that is my authority.

Here we have, then, the final statement of his side of the case, made by Judge Holt, through the mouth of counsel, revised and corrected under the stress of the occurrences at the White House and the negatory attitude of the members of the Cabinet present on the spot. Stripped of the allegation that the record was laid before the Cabinet and voted upon by every member of the Cabinet, its affirmations, carefully confined to "the confidential interview" between the President and the Judge-Advocate, go no farther than that "the identical paper" was "before the President," when he signed the death warrant, and they had a conversation "on the subject."

"He wants no misunderstanding" and does "not intend there shall be any." The counsel in great detail relates how he came by his facts. "That is my knowledge and that is my authority." Of course it is open to everybody to believe, if he choose, that the talk of the Cabinet meeting and of the unanimous vote of its members against the petition, was a mere rhetorical exaggeration of a simple narrative of Holt relating the incidents of an interview between the President and himself, struck off by Judge Pierrepont in the full fervor of his eloquence; but, nevertheless, it remains true that the Judge-Advocate, until the catastrophe befell, was satisfied it should stand, rhetoric and all; because he "reiterated the same thing" on Saturday, *after* the counsel had concluded his statement, and on Monday the counsel continued his address all day without being advised of the necessity for any retraction.

Be this as it may, there is now, at the last, no appeal by the Judge-Advocate to the members of the Cabinet, all of whom were living, as witnesses to the President's knowledge of the petition of mercy. He abandons hope of corroboration from members of the Cabinet, and he takes his stand upon the single categorical affirmation, that the "identical paper" formed part of the record when the record was before the President in 1865.

And, singular as it may appear, this is the very thing that the President does not categorically deny; he only infers the contrary from the appearance of the record in 1867.

The single categorical negation of the President is that he

neither saw nor read the recommendation. And, singular as it may appear, this the Judge-Advocate does not categorically affirm; he leaves it to be inferred from his averment of the presence of the paper and a conversation on the subject.

In short, the statements of the two disputants are not contradictory. Both may be true. And, when we recollect the feeble state of health of the President at the time of the "confidential interview" and his mood of mind towards the distasteful task forced upon him in a season of nervous debility; when we recollect the mode and manner the Judge-Advocate adopted of writing out the death warrant; it will seem extremely probable that both statements *are* true. The President made no "careful scrutiny" of the record in 1865, or he would not have needed to do so in 1867. The Judge-Advocate, inspired by his master, would not be too officious in pointing out to the listless and uninquiring Executive the superfluous little paper. He might do his whole duty, by conversing on the subject of the commutation of the sentence of the one woman condemned, and, then, by so placing the roll of papers for the President's signature to the death warrant as to bring the modest "suggestion" of the five officers *"right before his eyes,"* though upside down. If the sick President did not carefully scrutinize the papers, was that the Judge-Advocate's fault? Nay, in writing out the death warrant in the inspired way he did, this zealous patriot may have felt even a pious glow, in thus lending himself as an instrument to ward off a frustration of Divine justice. Alas! one may easily lose one's self in endeavoring to trace out the abnormal vagaries of the "truly loyal" mind, at that period of hysterical patriotism.

After these incidents on the Surratt trial, and at the White House, there could be no more mystery about the recommendation to mercy. It was historically certain that such a document, or rather a "suggestion," did in fact emanate from the Commission, and was at some time affixed to the record. Left out of Pitman's official compilation, nevertheless it was there. The only question about it which could any longer agitate the people was, had it been suppressed? And this, unfortunately, was now narrowed down to a mere question of veracity between the President and his subordinate officer, as to what occurred at the Confidential Interview; and which, moreover, threatened to resolve itself into a maze of special pleading about the lack of attention, on the part of the Executive, and the duty of thorough explanation, on the part of the Judge-Advocate, in the delicate task of approving the judgment of a Military Commission.

Whether this unsatisfactory and ticklish state of the issue was the cause or not, nothing was done in consequence of these revelations of the Surratt trial. The President, indeed, plunged as he was in the struggle to get rid of Stanton, which finally led to his impeachment, and remembering his own remissness in not scrutinizing the papers before he signed the death-warrant, could have had but little inclination to provoke another conflict, on such precarious grounds, by attempting the removal of the incriminated subordinate of his rebellious Secretary. He kept possession of the record, however, long enough to subject it to a thorough inspection by himself and his advisers, for (as appears from the letter of the chief clerk already quoted) it was not returned to the Judge-Advocate-General's office until December, 1867.

The Judge-Advocate, on his part, remained likewise passive and displayed no eagerness for a vindication by a court of inquiry.

He pleads in 1873, as excuse for his non-action, that "it would have been the very madness of folly" for him "to expose his reputation to the perils of a judicial proceeding in which his enemy and slanderer would play the quadruple role of organizer of the court, accuser, witness and final judge." Forgetting the "history" he had told Mr. Pierrepont, and then withdrawn, in 1867, he actually claims that he "was not aware that any member of Mr. Johnson's Cabinet knew of his having seen and considered the recommendation," and that he "was kept in profound ignorance of" "this important information" "*through the instrumentality of Mr. Stanton*"!

But, were it credible that the Judge-Advocate "supposed," as he says, "that this information was confined to" the President and himself, (not even his master, Stanton, knowing anything of the petition), even in that case the "perils" of an investigation, which he affects to dread, were all on the side of his adversary. The necessity for the President of the United States, himself, to come forward as the one sole witness to his own accusation – especially when the charge involved an admission of his own delinquency, and was to be met by the loud and defiant denial of his arraigned subordinate – was enough, of itself, to deter the Chief Magistrate of a great nation from descending into so humiliating a combat.

But, to lay no stress upon this consideration, it must be manifest to any one acquainted with the state of public feeling at the time, that the single, uncorroborated testimony of the maligned, distrusted Andrew Johnson, branded as a traitor by the triumphant Republican party, on the eve of impeachment, a hostile army under his nominal command, Stanton harnessed on his back, unfriendly private secretaries pervading his apartments, and detectives in his bed-chamber; in support of such a "disloyal" charge, disclosing, as it was sure to be asserted, a latent remorse for the righteous fate of the she-assassin; would have been hailed in all military circles with derision. The popular, the eminently loyal, the politically sound Judge-Advocate, backed by Stanton, Bingham and Burnett, by his Bureau and his Court, by General Grant and the Army, had certainly nothing to fear.

But, though this hero of so many courts-martial appears to have had no mind for a dose of his own favorite remedy, he began, in his characteristic secret way, to collect testimony corroborative of his version of the confidential interview. He writes no letter to a single Cabinet officer. But, immediately after the close of the John H. Surratt trial (August 24, 1867), he writes to General Ekin reminding him of an interview, soon after the execution, in which he (Holt) mentioned that the President had seen the petition; and he obtains from that officer the information he sought. In January, 1868, he quietly procures from two clerks in his office, letters testifying to the condition of the record when it arrived from the Commission, when the Judge-Advocate took it to carry to the

President, and when he brought it back. It is needless to say that, though these clerks state that the page, on which the petition was written, and the page, on which the latter portion of the death-warrant was written, are "directly face to face to each other;" they do not notice that, when the death-warrant was signed, the page, on which the petition was written, must have been, either under the other pages of the record, or upside down.

In this same month, the resolution of the Senate refusing to concur in the suspension of Stanton was adopted (January 13th, 1868). General Grant, the Secretary of War *ad interim*, in violation of his promise to the President, as alleged by the latter, thereupon surrendered the office to the favorite War-Minister, who thus forced himself back among the confidential advisers of the President.

On the 21st of February, the President, with one last desperate stroke, removed him from office; and on the 24th, Andrew Johnson was impeached for this "high crime."

In the midst of his troubles, the President finds time to pardon Dr. Mudd (Feb. 8th), who soon returns to his family and friends.

The impeachment trial ends May 26th, the President escaping conviction by but one vote; and Stanton at last lets go his hold on the War office.

In December, 1868, the Judge-Advocate is privately seeking testimony from the Rev. J. George Butler, of Washington, the minister who attended Atzerodt in his last moments, whose letter of the 15th is most satisfactory on Johnson's belief in the guilt of Mrs. Surratt, but most unsatisfactory in regard to the petition of mercy.

On the 1st of March, 1869, among the last acts of his stormy administration, the President undid, as far as he could then undo, the work of the Military Commission by setting Arnold and Spangler free; O'Laughlin having died from the effects of the climate. Had the five officers of the Military Commission been permitted to exercise their power of mitigating the sentence of Mrs. Surratt, as they did in the cases of these men, or had the Executive granted their prayer for clemency; the President might have signalized the close of his term by a still more memorable pardon, and the mother, rescued from death by mercy, would have joined the son, rescued from death by justice.

During the four years of the first administration of President Grant, while Andrew Johnson was fighting his way back to his old place, among the people of Tennessee, the story of the suppressed recommendation ever and anon circulated anew with unquenchable vitality. The reappearance of Mudd, Spangler and Arnold, as free men; the "doubtful" death of Stanton, "with such maimed rites" of burial, as might "betoken the corse they follow, did with desperate hand Fordo its own life;" every incident connected in any way with the tragedy of the woman's trial and death, and every prominent event in the career of the men who had surrounded the illstarred successor of the murdered Lincoln in the awful hour of his accession, revived the irrepressible question; and the friends of Mrs. Surratt's memory, and the friends of Johnson, alike, each by their own separate methods, on every such opportunity, appealed and re-appealed to the public, asserting again and again the suppression of the plea for mercy, propagating what General Holt brands as "the atrocious accusation," or, as he elsewhere characterizes their actions, "for long years wantonly and wickedly assailing" the ex-Judge-Advocate. And yet, during all these years, the baited hero is silent. He lies low. As far as appears, he makes no further efforts to secure testimony. His friend and old associate, Bingham, is by his side, yet he makes no appeal to him. He keeps close by him the letters he has already secured to substantiate his own version of the confidential interview. But he seeks for no Cabinet testimony. His stern master in the War Department, after the acquittal of the President, lays down his sceptre, and then, though the deadliest enemy of Johnson, is allowed to die in silence. Seward lives on and is asked to give no help. The ex-Judge-Advocate still lies low.

At length came the appointed time.

William H. Seward died on the 12th day of October, 1872. On the 11th day of February, 1873, Gen. Holt makes his appeal for testimony from the officers of Johnson's first Cabinet, by letter to John A. Bingham, requesting him to furnish his recollections of the late Stanton and the late Seward. On March 30th, 1873, he writes to James Speed, Ex-Attorney-General, inclosing a copy of Bingham's reply. On May 21st, 1873, he writes to James Harlan, Ex-Secretary of the Interior, inclosing a copy of Bingham's reply. In July, 1873, he writes to General Mussey, once Johnson's private secretary; and, in August, armed with the answers of these correspondents and with the letters he had gathered in 1867 and 1868, and unprovoked by any revivification of the old charge, he rushes into the columns of the Washington *Chronicle* with his formidable "Vindication."

CHAPTER FOURTEEN
The Trial of Joseph Holt

On the threshold of his Vindication, Gen. Holt revives the discredited and apparently forgotten declaration made by Mr. Pierrepont on the trial of John H. Surratt, and stakes his whole case upon the establishment of the truth of the allegation that the petition for commutation, attached as it was to the record of the findings and sentences of the Military Commission, was the subject of consideration at a meeting of the Cabinet of President Johnson, and its prayer rejected with the concurrence of the members present at such meeting.

So long as the contention is limited to what took place during that momentous hour between the President and himself, "alone," with the light thrown upon it by the record including the endorsed death-warrant and the affixed paper, he exhibits a certain lack of confidence in the strength of his defense. For, although he prints the "circumstantial evidence," as he calls it, to sustain his own version of the "confidential interview" (consisting of the two letters from his former clerk, heretofore alluded to, and the letter from Gen. Mussey saying that the "acting President" told him of the recommendation "about that time"), he confesses it was not until he recently had secured certain testimony that the petition had been considered by officers of the Cabinet, that he at length felt his case strong enough to warrant a public challenge of his adversary, and himself justified in submitting it to the public.

In short, we have a sort of reversal of the position of six years before. *Then*, after having at first put forward the assertion that the petition was considered by the Cabinet, the Judge-Advocate summarily suppresses that branch of his case, and puts into the foreground the explicit asseveration of the identical paper being "right before the President's eyes" when he signed the death-warrant. "He wants no misunderstanding about that." *Now*, while he keeps in mind, it is true, this version of the confidential interview, he relegates it to the rear, and constitutes the Cabinet consideration the very citadel of his cause.

As to what takes place at a meeting of the Cabinet, its members of course are the first, if not the only, witnesses. And it is a matter of surprise that General Holt, so far as is apparent, never, in all these past years, applied to any one of them to substantiate so essential a part of his vindication. He states that he has always been satisfied that the matter must have been considered in the Cabinet, and adds that "from the confidential character of Cabinet deliberations" he has "thus far been denied access to this source of information." But he does not say when, or to whom, he applied for such "access," or how he had been "denied." It is certain, from what he says elsewhere, that he never applied to Stanton or to Seward; he admits in a subsequent communication that he never applied to McCulloch, Welles or Dennison; and, from the tenor of their letters now in reply to his, it appears he never applied before to Harlan or to Speed. And these are all the members of the Cabinet of President Johnson in July, 1865. Moreover, he does not, even now, in 1873, make application in the first instance to an ex-Cabinet officer. His first application is made to John A. Bingham, his old colleague in the prosecution of Mrs. Surratt, for Cabinet information in the shape of conversations with the two ministers, who, after so many years of unsolicited silence in life, are now silent, beyond the reach of solicitation, in death. And it is not until he has secured the desired information, which he would have us believe was entirely unexpected, that he is stirred up to the necessity of a public vindication of his character; and then he selects the two of the surviving ministers of the Cabinet, known to be hostile to the ex-President, as the objects of solicitation, sending them, as a spur to their recollections, the letter containing the reminiscences of his serviceable ally. But, by some fatality, the industrious inquirer takes nothing by his somewhat complicated manœuvre. The letters he produces from Cabinet officers afford him no assistance. Judge Harlan can recall only an informal discussion by three or four members of the Cabinet (Seward, Stanton, himself and probably Speed) of the question of the commutation of the sentence of Mrs. Surratt because of her sex; which, she being the one woman under condemnation, would surely arise in a tribunal of gentlemen, whether there was a recommendation or not, as in fact it did even among the stern soldiers of the Military Commission. But the writer, who, as Senator from the State of Iowa, had voted for the conviction of President Johnson, makes the positive declaration, that "no part of the record of the trial, the decision of the court, or the recommendation of clemency was at that time or ever at any time read in my (his) presence." He remembers, with undoubting distinctness, inquiring at the time whether the Attorney-General had examined the record, and was told that the whole case had been carefully examined by the Attorney-General and the Secretary of War; and he states that the question was never submitted to the Cabinet for a formal vote.

This letter is most significant, both for what it says and for what it refrains from saying. Its positive statement annihilates the story of a "full Cabinet" when "the vote of every member" was adverse, and indeed of any Cabinet meeting whatever, where the paper was present and considered – such a story as Judge Pierrepont first gathered from the "voice" of Holt; and the absence of all affirmation that the writer had either seen or heard of the recommendation, while he expressly states that it was never read in his presence (considering the occasion and object of the letter and the bias of the ex-Senator), warrants the conclusion that such a document was not mentioned at the informal Cabinet consultation he describes.

In any view, the letter furnishes no support to Holt's contention. The writer expressly negatives the presence of the record and the paper, and he does not affirm that such a petition was alluded to, in terms, in the discussion in the presence of the President; which he surely would have done, in aid of his sorely tried friend, if such had been the fact.

The Judge-Advocate fares even worse at the hands of the Ex-Attorney-General. Here is a man who knew, if any other member of the Cabinet except Stanton knew, whether the paper in question ever came up for discussion before the President in his Cabinet. He goes so far as to say that, after the findings and before the execution, he saw the paper attached to the record "in the President's office;" a statement which reminds us of another of the same elusive and evasive character (that the paper was "*before the President*"), and, like that, affirms nothing one way or the other as to the consciousness of the President of its presence.

And then he proceeds as follows:

"I do not feel at liberty to speak of what was said at Cabinet meetings. In this I know I differ from other gentlemen" (presumably an allusion to the Seward and Stanton of Bingham's letter), "but feel constrained to follow my own sense of propriety."

His friend's necessity would have been met by something less than a repetition of what was *said* at Cabinet meetings. He had only to tell whether he saw a certain paper (not in the President's office), but at a meeting of the President and his advisers, or knew of the recognition there of its mere existence – a revelation which would not have violated the most punctilious sense of official propriety; and he feels constrained to withhold the least ray of light upon so simple a question.

The witness "declines to answer."

Ten years after the present controversy, Judge Holt, feeling acutely this weak point in his vindication, again appeals to Speed, in the most moving tones, to break his unaccountable silence and rescue his friend's gray head from "the atrocious accusation," "known to him to be false in its every intendment," with which that perfidious monster, dead now eight years, and, (as Holt significantly quotes), "gone to his own place," sought "to blacken the reputation of a subordinate officer holding a confidential interview with him."

And, strange to say, Speed first neglects even to reply to Holt's repeated communications for six months, and then just opens his lips to whisper, "I cannot say more than I have said." He had offered in private (if we may credit Holt) to write a letter to his aggrieved friend, giving him the desired information, "but not to be used until after Holt's death;" a proposition quite naturally discouraged by Holt, who made this sensible reply: "that a letter thus strangely withheld from the public would not, when it appeared, be credited."

But, when repeatedly implored to spread "the desired information" before the public, he again declines to answer. James Speed would not tell the truth, when by telling the truth he might relieve his old friend in "the closing hours of his life" from a most damnable calumny, because, forsooth, "of his sense of propriety." He could not violate the secrecy of a Cabinet meeting, held nearly twenty years before; a secrecy which he had good reason to believe had already been broken, in the professed interest of truth, by three of his own colleagues, and, in the alleged interest of a most foul falsehood, by the President himself.

Before the Judge finally gives up his old associate as hopeless, he craftily points out to him a way by which the ex-Cabinet officer may give his testimony without violating the most punctilious sense of propriety, not only, but without departing one iota from the literal truth. Since his first letter, General Holt informs him: "I have learned that although you gained the information while a member of the Cabinet, it was not strictly in your capacity as such, but that at the moment I laid before the President the record of the trial, with the recommendation for clemency on behalf of Mrs. Surratt, you chanced to be so situated as to be assured by the evidence of your own senses that such petition of recommendation was by me presented to the President, and was the subject of conversation between him and myself." Does this mean that Speed was an unseen spectator of the confidential interview, and witnessed the writing of the death-warrant? At all events, for some reason, the ex-Attorney-General was afraid to accept this opportunity to equivocate.

Holt may well wonder at Speed's obstinate silence. He exclaims, "It is a mystery to me." It will be a mystery to every one, provided the black charge was false. But, on the hypothesis that the charge was true, that the paper was suppressed, either actually or virtually, there is no mystery.

Had Speed known that the paper was, not only *"before"* the President, but considered by him, either in or out of the Cabinet, it is beyond the limit of human credulity to believe, for a moment, that, with all possible motives to lead him to succor his friend, and with none to lead him to shield the character of his dead political foe, he would not have uttered the one decisive word in the controversy. And he comes as near doing so as he dares, evidently. He shows, in 1873, a yearning to help his old friend – a yearning so strong that we may be sure it was not the frivolous pretext of "official propriety" which constrained him, then, much less in 1883.

If he, too, as Holt said of Stanton, feared the resentment of the dethroned Johnson in life, he certainly could not have feared the resentment of Johnson's ghost after death.

He must be numbered among those who,

> With arms encumbered thus, or this head-shake,
> Or by pronouncing of some doubtful phrase,
> As, *"Well, well, we know;"*
> or *"We could, an' if we would;"* or
> *"If we list to speak;"* or *"There be, an' if they might;"*

"ambiguously give out" to know what they are sworn "never to speak of." If there was any oath-guarding "fellow in the cellarage," rest assured it was not the pale wraith of the hood-winked Johnson, but the blood-boltered spectre of his once wide-ruling Minister of War.

Amid such a dearth of direct explicit testimony of members of the Cabinet about a disputed Cabinet incident, it is curious and interesting to watch the assiduous ex-Judge-Advocate, with the most ingenious and industrious sophistry, attempt to extract corroboration from the statements of the two ex-Cabinet officers, whom he has induced to speak, where in truth no corroboration can be found.

After all his efforts, he is forced at last to fall back upon the single testimony of the one man without whose encouraging information he frankly informs us he would not have dared to come before the people, and upon whom he brings himself to believe he might safely rest his defense. That man is John A. Bingham, now, as once before, Special Assistant Judge-Advocate to Joseph Holt.

During the eight years which had elapsed since their crowning achievement of hanging a woman for the murder of Abraham Lincoln, these two men had lived, for a considerable portion of the time, in the same city. They were together in the contest over reconstruction and impeachment, standing in the front rank of the enemies of Johnson. They were both at the Capital during the trial of John H. Surratt, when the ghastly reminiscences of the trial of the mother along with seven chained men must have drawn the two military prosecutors into a most sympathetic union.

And yet when, in February, 1873, Joseph Holt sits down in Washington to write his letter of inquiry to John A. Bingham, then in the same city, he would have us believe that he had never before poured into the bosom of his old colleague his own sufferings over the frightful calumny so long poisoning the very air he breathed, never before told him his embarrassment over the difficulty to elicit evidence from Cabinet officials, never before besought his friend for his own powerful testimony on the side of his persecuted fellow-official.

He writes to his former assistant, as though the information were now communicated for the first time, that the President and he were alone when the record was presented and the death-warrant signed; that he had always been satisfied the petition was considered in a Cabinet meeting, but has hitherto been unable to obtain any evidence upon that point; and then, in an artless, ingenuous manner, as if putting the question for the first time, asks his correspondent whether or not he had had a conversation with William H. Seward, Secretary of State under President Johnson, in reference to the petition, and "if so, state as nearly as you may be able to do all he said on the subject;" with a like request as to Edwin M. Stanton, Secretary of War.

With a diviner's skill he selects the two members of the Cabinet who are then dead; and, not to disappoint him, Bingham, in a letter from Washington six days later, informs him that he has struck the two-fold mark. With the same apparent artlessness which characterizes the letter of inquiry, this useful advocate now, as if for the first time, discloses to his long-tried colleague, that he did indeed have a conversation with each of the eminent men he had hit upon, who are now, alas! dead.

Judge Bingham is a most willing witness. He relates with great circumstantiality that "after the Military Commission had tried and sentenced the parties" he "prepared the form of the petition to the President." He then gives the form thus prepared as he now recollects it (in which there are two significant mistakes); he states that he wrote it with his own hands, that General Ekin copied it, and the five signed the copy; as if all this particularity had any relevance to the question at issue, as if the point in dispute was the existence of the paper, and not its suppression at a critical moment after it was written. He affects to believe it necessary to state to his old colleague, that he "deemed it his duty to call the attention of Secretary Stanton to the petition, and did call his attention to it before the final action of the President" – as if it were among the possibilities, that the head of the War Department could in any case have overlooked so important a paper, much less that the imperious Chief of this very prosecution could have been kept in ignorance, one hour, of what was done by his tools.

The Special Assistant, however, at last comes to the point:

> After the execution, the statement to which you refer was made that President Johnson had not seen the petition for the com-

mutation of the death sentence upon Mrs. Surratt. I afterwards called at your office, and, without notice to you of my purpose, asked for the record in the case of the assassins. It was opened and shown me, and there was then attached to it the petition, copied and signed as hereinbefore stated.

Oh, what an artless pair of correspondents! The former Special Assistant tells the former Judge-Advocate how he played the detective on him to his friend's justification; "*without notice of my purpose*"!

Soon thereafter I called upon Secretaries Stanton and Seward, and asked if this petition had been presented to the President before the death-sentence was by him approved, and was answered by each of those gentlemen that the petition was presented to the President, and was duly considered by him and his advisers, before the death-sentence upon Mrs. Surratt was approved, and that the President and the Cabinet upon such consideration were a unit in denying the prayer of the petition; Mr. Stanton and Mr. Seward stating that they were present.

In weighing the credibility of this statement, so conclusive if true, two considerations should be borne in mind.

1. That we have here, not the testimony of either Seward or Stanton, but the testimony of a man who, if the paper was in fact suppressed, must have been a participant in the foul deed. For no one will believe, for a moment, that Joseph Holt would have dared to perpetrate, if he could, or could have perpetrated, if he dared, so unspeakable a wickedness, without the knowledge and coöperation of his fiery leader in the conduct of the trial.

2. If this decisive information was in the possession of Judge Bingham at so early a date as "soon after the execution," why had he not communicated it to his distressed partner while Stanton and Seward lived? He had taken pains to obtain it to meet the ugly stories that were even then circulating against the Judge-Advocate. He knew it at the time of the struggle at close quarters over the petition during the Surratt trial, and he must have been

cognizant of the fact, that for the lack of it, that officer had been forced to withdraw the allegation of a full Cabinet consideration of the petition, which he had at first prompted the counsel of the United States boldly and publicly to make.

After the trial the reports grew louder and louder, until it was everywhere said that Andrew Johnson habitually declared that he had never seen the paper. Holt ran hither and thither collecting testimony from all available quarters. Hear Holt himself: "Every time the buzz of this slanderous rumor reached him (Bingham) during the last eight years – which was doubtless often – his awakened memory must have reminded him that he held in his keeping proof that this rumor was false." Why did not his former assistant even relieve his tremendous anxiety by telling him that he had evidence which would blow the calumny into the air? General Holt, in a letter in reply to Bingham's, dated at Washington the next day, which he also prints in his Vindication, says, "It would have been fortunate indeed, could I have had this testimony in my possession years ago."

He calls its concealment "a sad, sad mockery." Yes; and why was Judge Bingham willing to perpetrate such a "mockery," and continue the "mockery" until Stanton's death, and then until Seward's death, which occurred only a few months before he at last enlightens his colleague? Can the most credulous of men believe that, during all these years, he was guilty of such cruelty as not even to whisper such welcome intelligence into the ears of his sorely distressed brother officer?

And what shall we say of William H. Seward?

If that great man told Judge Bingham in 1865 what the Judge, after Seward was dead, first says he did, why had William H. Seward kept silent so many years, and at last died and made no sign? He must have heard the charge, so infamous if false, and, if Judge Bingham be believed, he must have known it to be false.

He must have heard the statement of Judge Pierrepont in open court in 1867. He must have known of the President's sending for the record and of the explosion thereupon in the Department of War. Why did he not at that crisis come forward with the proof of which the Judge-Advocate was so dreadfully in need?

The Secretary of State could not have intrenched himself behind the inviolability of proceedings of Cabinet meetings, as did the over-scrupulous Attorney-General, because, according to Judge Bingham, he himself had betrayed the secret long before.

And why did not Judge Bingham force him to speak, or else make public his interview with him, while Seward was alive and could either affirm or contradict it?

No, these two eminent lawyers, yoked together as the common mark of what they call a "most atrocious slander," originating with a President of the United States, bruited about everywhere both in official and private circles, wait eight long years, and until after the death of the head of that President's Cabinet, from whose lips one of them at least had heard at its very inception a solemn refutation of the black lie, before they venture to proclaim it to the world.

Mr. Bingham admits in his letter that, in 1865, "he desired to make" the facts he had ascertained "public." Why did he not "make public" what Seward had told him, while Seward was living?

He furnishes no answer to this question, and until he does, his testimony on the matter is tainted with a most reasonable suspicion.

And, besides, what we know of the situation of the Secretary of State at the time of the execution of Mrs. Surratt, of his subsequent career, and of his lofty character as a man, is sufficient to stamp the account of Judge Bingham as incredible.

William H. Seward, one of the most distinguished statesmen of the era of the civil war, one of the most illustrious founders of the Republican party, and one of the most trusted advisers of Abraham Lincoln, remained in the Cabinet of Andrew Johnson until the close of his administration. He united in the pardon of Mudd, Spangler and Arnold. He stood by the President fearlessly in the dark days of the impeachment, and when the President had become the target of the daily curses of thousands of Seward's former political friends. Had he known that the accusation against

General Holt was false, and at the same time heard the daily reiteration of its truth from the lips of his Chief, he would not have remained an hour in the Cabinet of such a monumental slanderer. So far from allowing the ceremonial restraints of Cabinet rules to make him a silent accomplice in a foul falsehood, he would have proclaimed the truth, if necessary, even from the steps of the Capitol.

Mr. Seward, at the time of the execution of Mrs. Surratt, could have but barely recovered from the broken jaw and broken arm from which he was suffering, when he bore the savage assault of Payne, and from the grievous wounds which that mad ruffian inflicted. One of his sons was still incapacitated because of injuries from the same hand, and his wife died June 21st, 1865. It is not at all probable that, in such dolorous circumstances, he would be required to give close attention to a subject entirely outside of the duties of his department, and in which his personal feelings as a sufferer were so deeply involved. He said himself under oath to a Congressional Committee, "Having been myself a sufferer in that business, the subject would be a delicate one for me to pursue without seeming to be over-zealous or demonstrative."

In spite of the eight-years-embalmed testimony of a hundred Binghams, we would not believe that the uncomplaining victim of Payne voted to deny the Petition of Mercy.

While no attempt is made to explain the silence of Seward during his lifetime, or the silence of Judge Bingham himself regarding the information he got from Seward, this willing witness does give a most singular and perplexing explanation of his long silence regarding the information he got from Stanton.

He says (in the same letter), "Having ascertained the fact as stated, I then desired to make the same public, and so expressed myself to Mr. Stanton, who advised me not to do so, but to rely upon the final judgment of the people."

General Holt, in a subsequent article, states that Stanton "enjoined upon the Judge silence in reference to the communication."

We are called upon to believe that the Secretary of War,

at the very first interview with Judge Bingham, when, upon the theory of the truth of the information, there could have been no conceivable motive for its concealment, advised his inquiring friend to suppress a fact essential to the refutation of a despicable slander, blotting the fair name of a brother officer. Not only this; but that the Secretary continued the injunction of silence during all the years the terrible charge was being bandied about on the lips of men to the daily torment of the poor man so cruelly assailed. As General Holt says, "It was a deliberate and merciless sacrifice of me, so far as he could accomplish it."

And he "enforced" the "silence" up to the day of his death.

But we ask what reason had the "Great War Minister" "to perpetrate so pitiless an outrage?" Why, in the days of the trial of John H. Surratt, why, in the days of his stern enmity towards the President, when his removal furnished the main ground of impeachment, did he not once speak out for his slandered servant, or even unlock the sealed lips of the obedient Bingham and suffer him to tell the truth?

General Holt, in 1883, on affirming in the text of his article that "Messrs. Seward and Stanton declared the truth to Judge Bingham," adds the following explanatory note:

> This praise was certainly due to Mr. Seward, but not, in strictness, to Mr. Stanton, since on making the communication to Judge Bingham, he endeavored and successfully, to prevent him from giving it publicity.
>
> The fear of Andrew Johnson's resentment, added to a determination on his part to leave my reputation – then under fire from his silence – to its fate, sufficiently explain his otherwise inexplicable conduct.

But does it? Is this in truth a sufficient explanation?

Stanton, the stern War Minister, fear the resentment of Andrew Johnson! When was he taken with it? When he bearded the President in his Cabinet? When he defied him in the War Department, and scattered his missive of removal to the winds? Or did he wait to begin to fear him until the President retired to private life, just escaping conviction by impeachment, and shorn of all popularity North or South? The preposterous nature of the cause assigned casts suspicion upon the assignor himself. As to the second cause, we are at a loss to conceive why Mr. Stanton should harbor such motiveless malignity against the reputation of his former colleague, then his pliant subordinate, and always his friend. We need, in this regard, an explanation of the explanation. If it be true, it settles the character of Stanton for all time.

But, it appears, in the words of General Holt, that "while he (Stanton) lived, this enforced silence was scrupously obeyed." Again we ask why?

Why should Bingham have obeyed the "advice," even if given by Stanton so long before? Why should the associate of Holt, in the prosecution and execution of Mrs. Surratt, have ministered to the malignity of Stanton, scrupulously obeyed his base injunction, and never even told his beloved fellow-laborer on the field of courts-martial, that he possessed such secret sacred testimonials in his favor?

The General gives us no explanation of this "inexplicable conduct."

Surely, the undaunted Bingham, who, as manager on the impeachment trial, so clawed the character of the arraigned President, could have had no "fear of the resentment of Andrew Johnson." And, unless the masterful Stanton held some secret back to feather his "advice," or lend weight to his injunction of silence, we see no reason why the fear of Stanton should have closed the lips of the voluble Special Judge-Advocate. He surely could not have joined in the fine irony of the Secretary, that it would be better for their mutual friend, although "under fire," "to rely on the judgment of the people."

But another, and a final, explanation is necessary. The Great War Minister died in December, 1869. Holt more than hints that "Providence" shortened his life so that he should no longer "perpetrate so pitiless an outrage" as keeping Bingham's mouth shut.

Why, then, do we hear nothing from Judge Bingham for

three years more? In the words of Holt, "after the Secretary had, amid the world's funeral pomp, gone down into his sepulchre, the truth came up out of the grave to which he had consigned it," and was "resurrected and openly announced by Judge Bingham." But why was the resurrection delayed until February, 1873? He does not tell us. Why should "the buzz of this slanderous rumor" (to use Holt's own words), "sadly recall to him that, though holding that proof, he was not yet privileged to divulge it?" There is no answer to this; none. The "scrupulosity" of Bingham did not end with the providential taking off of Stanton, but prolonged its reverential obedience to the advice of the dead, until his great colleague also was summoned from the scene.

Such resurrected truth, like the suggested letter of Speed to be used only after poor Holt's death, seems doubly obnoxious to the latter's own common sense remark: "thus strangely withheld from the public, it would not, when it appeared, be credited."

On the whole, it is exceedingly doubtful whether Judge Bingham's testimony does not do more harm than good to General Holt's case. It is the testimony of an accomplice, if the charge it is meant to refute is true. Its subject-matter is hearsay, withheld, so long as the direct evidence was attainable, for no good reason, or for a reason assigned which will not stand a moment's examination.

This interchange of letters between two associates in infamy, if infamy there were, the one applying for, and the other disclosing ostensibly for the first time, at so late a day, decisive information, which, in the ordinary course of things, the one must have asked for or the other revealed, and both talked over from the beginning, wears upon the face all the features of a collusive correspondence.

No one acquainted with the facts can be induced to credit what both these men state upon the threshold of their correspondence, and upon the truth of which their credibility is staked for all time, that, if two such conversations with Judge Bingham actually took place, this co-victim of a common charge would ever have withheld all knowledge of such important testimony from his brother in affliction for eight years, and until the lips of his two eminent interlocutors, whose confirmation would have at once and for ever crushed the calumny, were closed in death.

And, with this incontrovertible assertion, we dismiss John A. Bingham to keep company with Richard Montgomery and Sanford Conover, two witnesses who were once the subjects of his own fervid eulogy.

Another aspect of the case must for a moment detain us.

Under the admitted fact that the President approved the death-sentence on Wednesday, July 5th, it is by no means clear how we are to find room for this supposed Cabinet meeting.

The natural construction of Bingham's letter would lead us to believe that the Cabinet meeting, which the two Secretaries are said to have described, was a regular consultation between "the President and his advisers," held *before* the "confidential interview" at which the President "approved the death-sentence;" and that the entire Cabinet voted on the question raised by the petition, because it was "a unit in denying the prayer." This is but another version of the "full Cabinet" of Judge Pierrepont's first statement, and forcibly suggests that the two have an identical origin – at first withdrawn under compulsion while Seward lived, at last brought forward again after his death.

And every one, on such construction, would expect to hear the voices of McCulloch, Welles and Dennison, still living in 1873, and accessible to the ex-Judge-Advocate.

He states in his "Refutation," that he "had satisfactory reasons for believing that they were not there;" but he could not have gathered those reasons from Judge Bingham or his letter, which really is only consistent with the presence of some, if not all, of the three; and it is naturally to be inferred he got them from the ex-members themselves in letters repudiating all knowledge of the petition – letters he takes care not to publish.

Again: the Cabinet meeting described in Judge Bingham's letter cannot be made to square with the meeting described in the letter of Judge Harlan. The former was a regular Cabinet meeting, the latter was an informal discussion by a few members of the Cab-

The Trial of Joseph Holt

inet. At the one, the petition was "duly considered," at the other, neither record nor petition was present. At the one, "a formal vote" was taken upon the "question as to Mrs. Surratt's case;" at the latter, her case "was never submitted to a formal vote."

But – not to dwell further on dispensable points – it is enough to say that *any* Cabinet meeting whatever, for the consideration of the petition, held *before* the President's approval of the death-sentence, is, on the admitted facts of the case, an impossibility.

Indeed Holt himself, when driven to the question, does not claim that there was. The record was in the custody of the Judge-Advocate from the 30th of June until that officer carried it to the President on the 5th of July, and during that interval the President was sick-a-bed. It was General Holt, as he himself states, who first "drew his attention to the recommendation," and "the President then and there read it in my (his) presence." And this was at the confidential interview on Wednesday, July 5th. There could have been no meeting of the President and his Cabinet at which the record and petition were present and discussed, "before the approval of the death-sentence;" which confessedly was done at the confidential interview.

When this impossibility was pointed out by Andrew Johnson, General Holt, in his "refutation," with great show of indignation, denounces such an argument as "intensely disingenuous." While conceding at once that from the adjournment of the Commission to the 5th of July, the President "had been sick in bed, and had, of course, had no opportunity of conferring with any members of his Cabinet;" he proceeds to show what his idea of intense ingenuousness is, by claiming that what "Messrs. Seward and Stanton" (of Bingham's letter) "clearly meant was, that before the President had *finally* and *definitely* approved the sentences in question," the recommendation to mercy "had been considered by him and his advisers in Cabinet meeting;" and therefore such a meeting might have been held *after* the signature to the death-warrant, say on Wednesday afternoon (5th), or on Thursday, the 6th. And he, now, once again, as in the days of the Surratt trial, abandons allidea of a "full" or regular Cabinet meeting, and endeavors, with the most transparent sophistry, to identify the informal discussion of Judge Harlan's letter with the Cabinet Council of Judge Bingham. But alas! for the ingenuous General! Circumstances are too strong for him. For there is no more room for a Cabinet meeting, formal or informal, to do what Judge Bingham's informants are said to relate – i.e., consider, and then vote upon the petition – *after* the confidential interview than *before*.

It is agreed on all hands that the President approved of the death-sentence on Wednesday, at the confidential interview between Holt and himself, and, at that very time, and by the same warrant, appointed Friday the 7th, for the executions. The whole matter was begun and ended in an hour.

There was neither opportunity, nor, if there had been, use, to hold a Cabinet consultation upon the question of commutation after that.

The President had reviewed the record, and, without consultation with any human being but Holt, put his name to the death-warrant. Why consult his confidential advisers after he had decided the whole matter? Holt himself says that, at this private interview, it was not he, but Andrew Johnson, who had fully made up his mind that Mrs. Surratt must be put to death; that the President needed no urging or advice on that subject; that he inveighed against the women of the South with a ferocity which reminds us of the loyal Bingham himself. Holt says that the President himself, without a suggestion from him, was "prompt and decided" "as to *when* the execution should take place," "and in the same spirit too, in which he subsequently suspended the writ of Habeas Corpus, he fixed the Friday following." Why call in his "advisers" after he had, with the approval of his judgment and his conscience, put his hand to the work of blood! Besides, if he needed such a supererogatory endorsement of his "advisers," there was no time to get it.

The record with the death-warrant went direct to the Adjutant-General's office that very Wednesday. Holt cannot remember whether he took it or not, nor can the Adjutant-General remember when or how he received it. But this is of no consequence. The order for the execution was drawn on that day, the necessary copies made that day; it was promulgated on the morning of Thursday the 6th, and on that day at *noon*, the warrant for her death, within twenty-four hours, was read to the fainting woman in her cell. All day long, on the 6th, the White House was besieged by her friends, her priests and her daughter, to obtain a reprieve. The guardians of the President had no time to hold Cabinet consultations over foregone dooms of death. They were too busy intercepting verbal prayers for mercy, holding shut the doors of the President's private room, sending away all petitioners, for a few more hours' life, to the merciful Judge-Advocate, making sure that there should be four pine coffins and four newly dug graves, and that the Habeas Corpus should not leave one empty. Hold a Cabinet meeting after the President had signed the bloody warrant, and Stanton had once clutched it! Reopen the perilous question to hear Welles and Dennison, and McCulloch and Seward, to say nothing of Harlan and Speed and Stanton, discuss a petition addressed to the President who had already denied it! "Five members of our court have been suborned by their feelings to swerve from their duty. We run no more risks of soft-hearted gallantry this time amid the members of the Cabinet. Let the funeral games begin."

The ex-Judge-Advocate insists that the signature to the death-warrant was a matter of very little moment. The President could withdraw it at any time. But would he have us believe that, after the President had dispatched such a fatal missive to the officer whose sole duty, with regard to it, consisted in the promulgation of an order for its execution within twenty-four hours, such action was simply provisional and, according to usage, still subject to rescission by a Cabinet vote?

Desperate, indeed, must be the necessities of a defence, which drive the defendant on the forlorn hope of identifying a Cabinet meeting, voting as a unit to deny a petition for clemency, "*before the death-warrant was approved*," with a Cabinet discussion of the petition, *after* the death-warrant, fixing the execution on the next day but one, had been signed by the President (who is represented as urgent and eager at the moment of his signature to exact in the shortest time the extremest penalty); on the ground that the latter was held *before* the theoretical *animus revocandi* of the Executive had become technically inoperative with the last sigh of the condemned.

It has been suggested by one of his subordinate officers that the Secretary of War having seen the petition as soon as the record came to his department, it is inconceivable that, at some moment between the 30th and the 7th, the matter should not have been discussed by him with the President.

Of course, there can be no doubt that Stanton knew all about the recommendation. But, (and this obvious answer seems to have altogether escaped the attention of his friend), if the paper was in fact suppressed, it was suppressed with Stanton's own knowledge. Indeed, his must have been the master-hand. He it was who kept the late Vice-President up to the mark of severity as long as the bloody humor lasted.

He was the sovereign, and Bingham and Holt but his vassals. Everybody will give them the credit of not having dared to dream of suppression without the electrifying nod of their imperious lord.

And, from the long silence of one, if not both, of his slaves, it would appear, that he not only directed the suppression of the paper, but was too proud to deny, or suffer his minions to deny, it to his dying day.

CHAPTER FIFTEEN
Andrew Johnson Signs Another Death Warrant

Let us turn from the case made by General Holt, which on a cursory inspection seems so strong, but the seeming strength of which, on a closer scrutiny, dissipates itself among such perplexing questions, and lands us at last in the "enjoined silence" of Stanton, to the first public, authoritative charge made by the ex-President.

It appeared, November 12th, 1873, in the same newspaper which had published General Holt's Vindication, to which it was a reply. For it must be remembered that it was Joseph Holt, for eight years the accused, and not Andrew Johnson, for eight years the accuser, at the bar of rumor, who first threw down his gage in the public arena, defying his secret antagonist to come forth.

The gallant knight chose his own good time; and, at last, surrounded with sponsors, both clerical and martial, with banners flying and a most sonorous peal of trumpets, he burst into the lists, as though he would fain hope by noise and show to over-awe his dreaded adversary into submissive silence.

His thunders availed nothing. His glove had no sooner reached the ground than it was taken up.

Let us hear the plain, straightforward statement of Andrew Johnson. There are no mysteries to unravel, no explanations to explain.

> The findings and sentences of the court were submitted on the 5th of July (he and I being alone), were then and there approved by the Executive, and taken by the Judge-Advocate-General to the War Department, where on the same afternoon the order to carry them into effect was issued. Mr. Speed, doubtless, saw the record, but it must have been in the Department of War, and not in the Executive office.

After thus quietly disposing of Mr. Speed's evidence, he proceeds:

> The record of the court was submitted to me by Judge Holt in the afternoon of the 5th day of July, 1865. Instead of entering the Executive Mansion in the usual way, he gained admission by the private or family entrance to the Executive office. The examination of the papers took place in the library, and he and I alone were present. The sentences of the court in the cases of Herold, Atzerodt and Payne, were considered in the order named, and then the sentence in the case of Mrs. Surratt. In acting upon her case no recommendation for a commutation of her punishment was mentioned or submitted to me.

He then states that the question of sex was discussed alone; Holt insisting upon carrying out the sentence without discriminating as to sex; that a woman unsexed was worse than a man; that too many females had abetted traitors during the war, and that there was a necessity an example should be made.

> He was not only in favor of the approval of the sentence but its execution on the earliest practicable day.
> Upon the termination of our consultation, Judge Holt wrote the order approving the sentences of the Court. I affixed my name to it, and, rolling up the papers, he took his leave, carrying the record with him, and departing as he had come through the family or private entrance.

And there we must leave him.

True, he rejoined, in December, in another very long article, contributed to the same newspaper, in which he endeavored to break the force of several points made in Johnson's answer, and dwelt with much insistence on the abstention of the President from making any open charge against him, and on his adversary's present silence with regard to General Mussey's letter. But there is nothing new in the way of testimony, except two sympathizing letters from Generals Ekin and Hunter, respectively; the former of which might be construed by the uncharitable as evidence that General Holt, at the time of the execution, was already forestalling anticipated accusation by defending himself in private to his friends; the latter is a tribute from the grim President of the Military Commission to the Judge-Advocate's *tenderness* to the prisoners before that body, of which the printed record of the trial affords such striking illustrations.

This lengthy "Refutation," as it was entitled, upon the whole added little, if any, strength to the "Vindication." His accuser, on his side, resting content with his one single explicit public utterance, paid no attention to it.

And when, at the present hour, we calmly survey the relative standing, the position, the character and career of the two combatants, the circumstances surrounding the momentous confidential interview, the silent testimony of the record with the significant twist of the death-warrant, the nature of the accusation, the mysteries enveloping the belated defense, the probable motives actuating each, the thirst for blood which for a time maddened the leading spirits of the War Department, the passivity of Johnson for the few weeks after his sudden and sombre inauguration, and for the same period the wild and reckless predominance of Stanton – what valid reason exists why we should discredit, or even suspect for a moment, the veracity of the ex-President? Andrew Johnson looms up in history a very different figure from the one discerned by his enemies, both North and South, amid the passions of his epoch. He was no inebriate, as he was stigmatized because of the unfortunate incident at his inauguration as Vice-President. He was no weak, frightened tool, as he appeared to be at the bloody crisis of his accession to the Presidency. He was no apostate from his section, as he was cursed by the South for being at the breaking out of the war. He was no traitor to the North, as he was denounced by the impeachers for the mere endeavor to carry out the reconstruction policy of his lamented predecessor. He was not the garrulous fool, he was called in ridicule when he "swung around the circle." He is now recognized, when his career is reviewed as a whole, as a man temperate in his habits, firm, self-willed and honest; as a statesman, intelligent though uncultured, sometimes profound and always sincere; and as a union-loving, non-sectional, earnest patriot. His impeachment is looked back upon by the whole country with shame. His impeachers are already, themselves, both impeached and convicted at the bar of history.

In sober truth, so unique and perfect a triumph never capped and completed the career of Roman warrior or modern ruler of men, as when, but little more than a year after his reply to General Holt, the ex-President – once again the chosen representative of that State whose rebellious people he had coerced with an iron hand as military governor during the Civil War – took his seat in that body, before which he had been arraigned on the impeachment of the House of Representatives and had escaped conviction by but a single vote.

With the words of Holt's denunciation still fresh in their remembrance, the citizens of Washington loaded the desk of the retributive Senator with flowers; and, when he advanced, amidst so many colleagues who had condemned him as judges, to take the oath of office, and again when, a few days later, his voice, which had before been heard pleading for the imperiled Union, was from the same place once more heard pleading for the imperiled Constitution, the crowded galleries and corridors gave him a conquering hero's welcome.

When in the following summer he died, his body was followed to its grave in the mountains by what it is hardly an exaggeration to call the whole people of his State. When Congress reassembled, the Senate and the House clothed themselves with crape. One of his former judges, who had voted him guilty of high crimes and misdemeanors (Morton, of Indiana), thus spoke of him in the Senate: "In every position in life he showed himself to be a man of ability and courage, and I believe it proper to say of Andrew Johnson that his honesty has never been suspected; that the smell of corruption was never upon his garments."

The same Senator related that when Johnson, as the newly appointed Military Governor, arrived at Nashville "he was threatened with assassination on the streets and in the public assemblies, but he went on the streets; he defied those dangers; he went into public assemblies, and on one occasion went into a public meeting, drew his pistol, laid it on the desk before him, and said: 'I have been told that I should be assassinated if I came here. If that is to be done then it is the first business in order, and let that be attended to.' No attempt having been made he said: 'I conclude the danger has passed by;' and then proceeded to make his speech."

Again the Senator said, "After I had voted for his impeachment, and met him accidentally, he wore the same kindly smile as before, and offered me his hand. I thought that showed nobility of soul. There were not many men who could have done that."

The man, of whom two such incidents could be truthfully related, could never have invented so foul a charge against an innocent subordinate.

A Senator from a neighboring State (McCreery), on the same mournful occasion said of him:

> When he went to Greeneville he was a stranger, and a tailor's "kit," his thimbles and his needles, were probably the sum-total of his earthly possessions; at his death, the hills and the valleys and the mountains and the rivers, sent forth their thousands to testify to the general grief at the irreparable loss.
>
> I honor him for that manly courage which sustained him on every occasion, and which never quailed in presence of opposition, no matter how imposing. I honor him for that independence of soul which had no scorn for the lowly, and no cringing adulation for the exalted. I honor him for that sterling integrity which was beyond the reach of temptation, and which, at the close of his

public service, left no blot, no stain upon his escutcheon. I honor him for that magnanimity which after the war cloud had passed, and the elements had settled, would have brought every citizen under the radiant arch of the bow of peace and pardon.

Another Senator (Paddock, of Nebraska) gave utterance to the following unchallenged statement:

> I believe, sir, notwithstanding the fact that a painful chapter relating to the official acts of Andrew Johnson was made in this very chamber, that no Senator here present will refuse to-day to join me in the declaration that he was essentially an honest man; aye, sir, a patriot in the fullest sense of the term.

Yet another (Bogy, of Missouri), said:

> His last election to a seat on this floor as Senator was the work of his own hands, brought about by his own indomitable will and pluck, the reward of a long and terrible contest, continuing for seven years, unsuccessful for a time, and appearing to all the world besides himself as utterly hopeless; nevertheless, finally he was triumphant. From what I have learned from those who are familiar with this, his last contest, he exhibited more openly his true and peculiar nature, than at any other period of his life – which was to fight with all his might and all his ability, asking no quarter and granting none; and although like bloody Richard now and then unhorsed, still to fight and never surrender, until victory perched upon his banner.

Senator Bayard said, "Friend or foe alike must admit his steady, unshaken love of country; his constant industry; his simple integrity and honesty; his courage of conviction, that never faltered."

Truly, the solemn word of a man, of whom such things can be said, is no light thing – to be thrust aside by windy abuse or vociferous denial.

Now, what conceivable motive had such a man, seated in

the chair of the Chief Magistracy of this republic, surrounded by Cabinet officers who had been the advisers of his predecessor, to invent, in the first place, so horrible a story as that a friendly subordinate officer had deliberately, in a case of life and death, suppressed so vital a document? For it is contradictory of historical fact, that he never openly made the charge until the year 1873.

This may be true of the period from about the time of the execution up to the disclosures of the John H. Surratt trial in 1867. But our review of the incidents of that trial, which General Holt in his refutation seemed to have totally forgotten, proves, beyond the possibility of controversy, that the President then first thought himself driven to inspect the record to ascertain the existence of such a paper, and then first, after the discovery that there was in fact a recommendation, at once, and at all times afterwards, openly asserted that he had not seen it or read it. Every one around him knew that he so said. Stanton, his great enemy, Seward, his great friend, knew it. Bingham, at the very beginning when Stanton forbade him to refute it; Bingham, when Butler pierced his shield in the House of Representatives, and Bingham, when at the bar of the Senate as manager of the impeachment he belabored his old-time Commander-in-Chief, knew it; Holt, when he delivered his contradiction through Judge Pierrepont to the Surratt jury, and when he felt the shadows darkening over his head because of the "inexplicable conduct" of the great War Minister in "perpetuating the pitiless outrage," knew it, and recognized the President of the United States as the responsible author of the tremendous accusation.

If Holt is to be credited, the President must have known that four at least of his confidential advisers stood ready to shatter the baseless calumny. What conceivable motive, we ask again, to invent such a story – so easy of refutation, so ruinous to himself, if refuted?

The necessity to make some reply to this pressing question seems to have driven both General Holt himself and his defenders into the maintenance of the most absurd, antagonistic and untenable positions.

Holt's theory on this subject in his "Refutation" is even ingenious in its absurdity. He would have us believe that when Johnson originally fabricated the calumny, "he had not yet broken with the Republican party, and was, doubtless, in his heart at least, a candidate for reëlection," of course by that party. If this is true, then the "fabrication" was made before the fall of 1865, for by that time the President was in full swing of opposition to the men who had elected him Vice-President. During this brief transitory period, according to Holt, Johnson discovered that the hostility of the Catholics (especially, as may be inferred, those of the Republican party), on account of his signature to the death-warrant of Mrs. Surratt, would blast this otherwise felicitous prospect. Accordingly, to abate this uncomfortable hostility, this Republican candidate concocted the vile slander and set it secretly and anonymously circulating among his friends and followers – even his greed for reëlection being not strong enough to give full effect to his cowardly policy by openly clearing his own skirts. Could the fatuity of folly farther go? The dream of Andrew Johnson as a Republican candidate for President had ceased to be possible even before the execution of Mrs. Surratt. The Catholics who could be conciliated by any such story might be numbered on Johnson's fingers. And the undisguised signature to the death-warrant could be obliterated by no plea of abatement which the petitioner dared not avow.

On the other hand, the other suggestion put forward, if not by Holt himself; by several of his defenders, viz.: that the President propagated the lie "to curry favor with the South in the hope to be elected to the Presidency," has the one merit of being in direct antagonism to the foregoing theory, but nevertheless is yet more flimsy and preposterous. At the time he invented the story, if invention it was (as Holt appears to have perceived), the road to the Presidency was to curry favor with the North and not with the down-trodden South. And after Johnson had escaped conviction and removal by but one vote, and had retired from office execrated by the North and distrusted even yet by the South, the chance of the Presidency for such a character as he was popularly considered then – especially by truckling to the discredited South – could only look fair in the imagination of a lunatic.

No Southern man has seriously thought of being, or has been seriously thought of as, a candidate for President of either political party since the termination of the war, let alone the one Southerner reputed to have been false alternately to both parties and both sections.

Besides, Andrew Johnson never apologized for his appointment of the Military Commission, for his approval of its judgment, or for his signature to the death-warrant. He pardoned Dr. Mudd on the very eve of the Impeachment Trial. And he pardoned the two remaining prisoners just before he went out of office. And he may, therefore, be held to have thus signified his reawakened reverence for constitutional rights as expounded in the Milligan decision.

But in no other way did he ever acknowledge that in taking the life of Mary E. Surratt he had done wrong. On the contrary, he defended his action in his answer of 1873, and he justified his denial of the habeas corpus, which the ex-Judge-Advocate had the exquisite affrontery to cast up against him. That a President in his situation could cherish aspirations – or hope – of reëlection, based on such a phantom foundation as the whining plea that he would have commuted the unlawful sentence of a woman, hung by his command, to imprisonment for life, had he been permitted to see the petition of five of her judges – such an imputation can only be made by men mad enough to believe him to have been the accomplice of Booth and Atzerodt.

Finally, let us sternly put the question: What right has Holt to ask us, on the word of himself and his associates, to reject the testimony of Andrew Johnson, who at the best was their accomplice or their tool? He, and his associates, demanded the life of Atzerodt for barely imagining the death of so precious a Vice-President. He, and his associates, hounded the woman to the scaffold, welcoming with delight the stories of spies, informers, personal enemies, false friends, against her, and meeting with contumely and violence the least scrap of testimony in her favor. He suppressed the "Diary." Why may he not have been bad enough to suppress the recommendation? Two of the same band of woman-stranglers kept back from the President the petition for mercy, which wailed out from the lips of the stricken daughter. Why should he not have kept back the timorous suggestion of five officers, who were so soft-hearted as to "discriminate" as to sex? His fate will be – and therein equal and exact justice will be done him – to go down through the ages, stealing away, in the dusk of the evening, from the private entrance of the White House, bearing the fatal missive – the last feeble hope of the trembling widow crushed in his furtive hand.

CHAPTER SIXTEEN
Conclusion

That the petition for commutation was a device of the Triumvirate of prosecutors to secure the coveted death-sentence, employed in reliance upon the temporary ascendency of the chief of the three over the beleaguered President, and upon the momentary pliability, heedlessness, or, it may be, semi-stupefaction of the successor of the murdered Lincoln, to smother the offensive prayer: such an hypothesis alone seems adequate in any degree to reconcile the apparent contradictions, clear up the perplexities and solve the mysteries, which hang around this dark affair.

It furnishes the only rational answer to the else insoluble question, how it happened that a court, a majority of whose members had the inclination and the power to lower the punishment of the solitary woman before them to life-long imprisonment, as the court did with the three men who were tried with her and convicted of the same crime, did nevertheless, by at least a two-thirds vote, condemn her to die by the rope.

It lights up the else inscrutable prohibition by Stanton of a public exculpation of his subordinate officer, softened by the sardonic admonition "to rely" for justification "on the final judgment of the people." A source of glorification, rather, it should be, that no maudlin pity for a woman had been suffered to intercept the death-stroke of a righteous vengeance.

It accounts for the "scrupulous obedience" of Bingham, not only until Stanton's death, but three years after, until Seward, too, had gone. Stanton knew the petition had been suppressed or made invisible; Seward, that the petition never had been before the Cabinet.

It throws a glimmer, faint it is true, on the shameful attitude of Speed, eight years after the death of Johnson – still shutting his ears to the repeated appeals of his agonized friend, and still falling back on his propriety. According to Judge Harlan, the whole record had been examined by the Attorney-General, as well as the Secretary of War. Speed, too, under the spell of Stanton, may have fingered the obnoxious paper, which might nip the bloody consummate flower of his *"common law of war."*

It furnishes the only plausible reason why such an historic document did not appear in the published official record of the proceedings of the Military Commission, in November, 1865, or in the reports of the Judge-Advocate, first, to the President, and, second, to the Congress.

It illumines with a baleful light the atmosphere of sinister secrecy, in which this adjunct to the record, for no lawful reason, has been enshrouded; the mysterious incidents at the Surratt trial, such as the tardy and reluctant production, the faltering and imperfect exhibition, and the hasty withdrawal of the "roll of papers;" the two statements of Mr. Pierrepont; the shrinking of the "full Cabinet meeting" into a "confidential interview," until after Seward's death; and the singularly equivocal language that the petition was *"before the President"* when he signed the warrant.

And, finally, when it is considered that the suppression of the paper was not the overt act of any one man, but the result of a strictly formal presentation of the record on the part of the Judge-Advocate, aided, it may be, by a timely sleight-of-hand in writing the order of approval, and of a blind carelessness on the part of the President in the examination of the papers; this hypothesis goes far to explain the reluctance of General Holt to rest his defense on his own evidence of the confidential interview, his eager grasping after Cabinet corroboration, and the abstention of both Judge-Advocate and President from taking official action upon the charge, the one for vindication, the other for punishment.

* * * *

And so the history of this murder of a woman by the forms of military rule slowly unrolls itself, to disclose, as its appropriate finis, the writer of the death-warrant struggling in the meshes of his own fraud.

The draughtsman of the unaddressed petition for commutation, after waiting eight years for death to clear the way, comes to the help of his old colleague, only to be caught in the same net.

The entangled twain call up the sullen shade of their departed master, and force him to father the trick he fain would have scorned.

These three are the men who, when the summary methods of martial law would else have failed to crush out entirely the life of their victim, contrived to attain their bloody end by cool and deliberate chicanery.

The other actors on the scene may plead the madness of the time. For these three no such plea is open. They superadded to the common madness of the time the particular malice of the felon. Upon their three heads should descend the full weight of criminal turpitude involved in this most unnatural execution.

They sat upon the thrones of power. They dragged a woman from her humble roof and thrust her into a dungeon. They chose nine soldiers to try her for the murder of their Commander-in-Chief. They chained her to the bar along with seven men. They baited her for weeks with their Montgomerys and Conovers, their Weichmans and Lloyds, the spawn of their bureau, dragooned by terror or suborned by hope. They shouted into the ears of the court appeal on appeal for her head. And, when at last five of their chosen sons sickened at the task, and shrank from shedding a woman's blood, they procured the death-sentence by a trick. They forged the death-warrant by another. They turned thimble-riggers under the very shadow of the gallows. They cheated their own court. They cheated their own President. They cheated the very executioner. They sneaked a woman into the arms of death by sleight-of-hand. They played their confidence game with the King of Terrors. They managed to hide the cheat from the country until they quarreled with their new Commander-in-Chief. Then ensued an interval of ambiguous mutterings, dark equivocations, private accusation, private defenses. From one side: "I never saw the paper." From the other: "It was right before his eyes."

The twin ex-Judge-Advocates, at length, brace each other up to the sticking-point and venture on an appeal to the public. The ex-President, thus driven at bay, fulminates the secret infamy in all its foul extent to the whole world. Thereupon, Great Nemesis finds her opportunity, and makes these once high-placed, invulnerable woman-slayers the sport of her mighty hands.

Every one, as if coerced by some magic power, comes at last to act as though he were afraid of the other, and, willing or unwilling, contrives to show how profoundly base the others are.

Stanton slinks mysteriously into the shadow of death, refusing to cut his co-conspirator down from the gibbet where the dreaded Johnson has swung him. Bingham, standing like an Indian with a single female scalp bleeding from his girdle, presses his finger to his lips until Stanton and Seward die. Speed, with the obnoxious petition pressed again and again to his nostrils, feebly yet persistently refuses to open his mouth.

Holt pictures the dead Johnson exulting even in Hell over the silence of his old Attorney-General; blasts the character of Stanton by ascribing his injunction of silence to a motive the most diabolic; and, unconscious seemingly that he does it, at the same time ruins the credit of Bingham by extolling his "scrupulous obedience" to such an infernal command.

Johnson unwittingly proclaims the pardon of the slain woman in his anxiety to show that he signed her death-warrant through ignorance, forced upon him by the ineffable depravity of the men in whom he was compelled to trust.

This controversy over the petition of clemency was the only thing needed to round out and decorate the entire, complete and perfect iniquity of the whole drama. It is immaterial and indifferent to history where the truth lies between these combatants in so unsavory a strife. Each one tears off the burning brand of shame, not to extinguish it, but to pass it on to his colleague. If we credit Holt, it is difficult to conceive the malignity of soul of Andrew Johnson, who could invent so foul a charge, the meanness of spirit of Edwin M. Stanton, who, knowing its blackness, could forbid the promulgation of the truth, the cowardly silence of John A. Bingham, whose lips the death of the dreaded Stanton alone could unclose. If we credit Johnson, then in all the crowded catalogue of inquisitors, persecutors, cruel or pettifogging prosecuting officers, devil's advocates and murderous Septembrisers, there is not one who would not spurn with profane emphasis association with Holt or Bingham or Stanton.

As the choicest specimen in this shower of accusations and counter-accusations, listen to the tender-hearted ex-Judge-Advocate of 1873 – once the stony head of the death-dealing Bureau – rebuking Andrew Johnson for his cold-blooded cruelty!

> I would have shuddered to propose the brief period of two days within which the sentences should be executed, for with all the mountain of guilt weighing on the heads of those convicted culprits I still recognized them as human beings, with souls to be saved or lost, and could not have thought for a moment of hurrying them into the eternal world, as cattle are driven to the slaughter-pen, without a care for their future.

Listen again to the former expounder of the "common law of war" before the Military Commission, as he arraigns the ex-President for his disregard of the writ of habeas corpus:

> The object of which was, and the effect of which would have been, had it been obeyed, to delay the execution of Mrs. Surratt at least until the questions of law raised had been decided by the civil courts of the District; yet this writ was, by the express order of the President, rendered inoperative. And so, under this

Presidential mandate, the execution proceeded.... But for his direct intervention and defiant action on the writ, whatever might have been the final result, it is perfectly apparent her life would not then have been taken.

Once more. Hear J. Holt, the Recorder of the Commission!

As Chief Magistrate he was, under the Constitution [Hear Him!], the depositary of the nation's clemency and mercy to the condemned, and a pressing responsibility rested upon him as such *to hear the victims of the law before he struck them down.* [The italics are his who wrote out the death-warrant.] Did he do this? On the contrary, he gave... a peremptory order to admit nobody seeking to make an appeal in behalf of the prisoners, saying that he would "see no one on this business."

He closed his door, his ears, and his heart against every appeal for mercy in her behalf, and hurried this hapless woman almost unshrived to the gallows.

What a picture is this!

The minion of Stanton, the colleague of Bingham, the tutor of Weichman, the tutor of Lloyd, the procurer of the death-warrant, weeping over the empty grave in the Arsenal, which, after his master's relentless watch was over, had at length given up its dead!

Here we are forced to stop. After such an exhibition, we can linger no longer over this miserable scramble to shirk responsibility. Its only consequence of historic importance, after all, is the light it casts upon the memory of the sacrificial victim. Out of the cloud of mutual vituperation, which covers the men who, among them, somehow, compassed her slaughter, her innocence rises clearer and clearer, like the images of retribution from the foul fumes of the witches' cauldron.

Her vindication must be held to be final, complete and unassailable, when John A. Bingham is anxious to acquaint the country that he drafted a petition to save her life; when J. Holt pretends to weep for her; when Andrew Johnson is forced, by the inexorable pressure of events, to confess that when he signed her death-warrant he knew not what he did.

As we let fall the curtain at the close of this dark and shameful tragedy, let us endeavor to anticipate the verdict of history.

The execution of Mary E. Surratt is the foulest blot on the history of the United States of America.

It was a violation of the most sacred provisions of that Constitution, whose enforcement was the vaunted purpose of the War.

It was a violation of the fundamental forms and principles of criminal jurisprudence, centuries older than the Constitution.

It was a violation of that even-handed justice, which is said to rule in the armies of Heaven and among the inhabitants of the earth.

It was a violation of those chivalrous impulses which spring unbidden to the manly breast in the presence of woman.

It was a violation of the benign precepts of Jesus, which enjoin tenderness to the fatherless and the widow.

It was a violation of the magnanimity of the brave soldier, which scorns to wound the weak, the fallen and the helpless.

It was a violation of even the common instincts of fairness, which subsist, as a matter of course, between man and man.

It was unconstitutional. It was illegal. It was unjust. It was inhumane. It was unholy. It was pusillanimous. It was mean. And it was each and all of these in the highest or lowest degree. It resembles the acts of savages, and not the deeds of civilized men.

The annals of modern times will be searched in vain to furnish its parallel. Execrations rise to our lips, as we read, in the pages of Macaulay, of the hanging of Alice Lisle, and the burning of Elizabeth Gaunt. But Alice Lisle and Elizabeth Gaunt were indicted by grand juries, tried by petit juries, found guilty, and sentenced, in strict accordance with criminal procedure. The forms of law, which the bigoted James, and even the infamous Jeffrey, were careful to observe, were swept aside by Holt and Bingham and Stanton, with a sneer.

We turn aside with sickening horror from the recital of the murderous orgies of the Terrorists of the French Revolution – shedding the blood of the young, the tender, the beautiful, the brave. But the Terrorists of France could plead the excuse, that they were driven to madness by the thought, that the invading hosts, encompassing the new-born Republic, were drawing nearer and nearer, every hour, with vengeance and counter-revolution perched upon their banners; and a merciful destiny granted them the grace to expiate their bloody deeds on the same scaffold as their victims.

But, in the case of Mary E. Surratt, not a single redeeming feature relieves "the deep damnation of her taking off."

Alas! Alas! Right in the centre of the glory which beams from the triumph of the Union and Emancipation, there hangs a dark figure – casting an eclipsing shadow – ever widening – ever deepening – in the eyes of all the coming generations of the just.